Copyright © 2022 Genevieve L. Hughes

Push

EVIE CAMPBELL

A READER'S TALE, BOOK 1

Non Content Warning

We don't do those here, they're detrimental to the plot; if you really can't live without them turn the page. This satirical parody mocks Indie publishing/promotion; it is not factual, nor is it a how-to book. Liberties were taken.

Brief terms for reference—this is not book padding or a scam, terminology may be found in the glossary.

Please research unfamiliar words via your ebook lookup (Web/dictionary). Readers are smart; don't underestimate them.

The author is Australian, so please forgive them for any unfamiliar phrases used.

Content Warning

Warnings for: Online bullying, mental health, off-screen self-harm. No cheating (except book boyfriends). Slow-burn, dual POV with flashbacks. If timelines and diaries jar your sensibilities, skip this read.

Dedication

To the Indie bloggers who exposed the corruption in beauty: you broke some, but strengthened and forged steel in others.

A fresh edit means it's time to turn up the snark. Thanks for taking a peek into our manically entertaining world.

One song captures PuSh: "Secrets" by OneRepublic.

To the unseen: We see you.
To my girls: You know who; this is yours.
You can't incite hate without fallout—Evie.

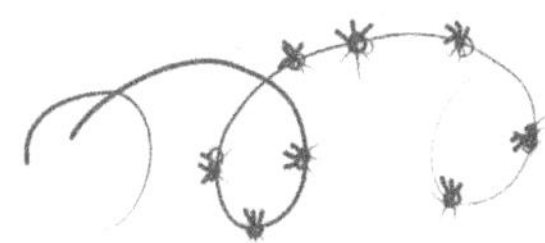

Cover: GLH
Cover design: GLH
Original background cover photo, Irises: GLH.
Original vectors: GLH
Chessboard: Deposit Photos
Typography: Licensed by Canva

A catalogue record for this book is available from the National Library of Australia

Synopsis

What if everything you've—
Purchased. Read. Shared.
In the past three years was—
Fake. Recycled. Tainted.
Would you one-click hot promos?
Scrutinize content?
Hunt familiar plots/quotes?
We did.
Buckle up—it's time to ride.
Strap on your armor-plated big girl panties; we're getting messy.
Welcome to Indie publishing.
Welcome to #smutmafiagate.

<h1 style="text-align:center">Prologue</h1>

Kat's notebook:

XYZ—outline/notes, random thoughts 3/18/21.

Welcome to Romancelandia, and indie publishing at its best.

The book community, as a whole, is sweet; people are united by words, desperate to escape their dreary daily lives, between well-worn pages of novels.

Stories older than the majority of readers, flood romance-hungry minds and feed emotion. They magically take us to worlds we will never travel, living vicariously through another's words. Our imagination fuels desire, a drive for acceptance, comfort, and love—often supplemented by fictional book boyfriends.

Reading offers escapism, familiarity, and connection. Books are a precious blanket in times of heartache and happiness–equally. We treasure those words in their many romantic forms, and defend our smut to the death.

Independent publishing's a fantastic opportunity for

anyone to share their story. It is accessible for all budgets, large or small. The author is an editor, account keeper, cover designer, and marketer if need be. Some troll online and prey on this new blood, pushing services they can ill afford. Others offer support for free, having been there and done it all the hard way. The big-name promotion companies, the best of the best, are selective—or should be. Too many were caught out in various 'gates' in the early years.

Education is key. A minute percentage of this close-knit community isn't healthy. Think acid bath, eating away flesh —toxicity beyond Chornobyl. It burns from the inside out, digesting energy with malicious intent.

Those are the voices readers hear.

As an outsider looking in, it appears to be pure insanity. This isn't how the rest of society behaves—perhaps a few–but not well-balanced, healthy human beings. The book population hierarchy pushing their agenda, in general, has become fake.

In recent years, a colossal influx of new authors created a social-media-driven madhouse. An aggressive and desperate breed arose from the tombs, as a virus suffocated the globe. Hatred spewed forth—sparks of secrets hidden, briefly came to light, only to be snuffed out. The layers of protection, on and offline, hid agendas. Beneath the veneer of an amazing, supportive community–a once prestigious and precious art form–a rotten and corrosive core was cultivated in darkness.

Delve deeper if you will, into reading teams, blogs, and reviewer lists. Innumerable, voluntary hours were wasted filtering friend requests, group invites, giveaways, and competitions. One-click purchases, ads, and instant messaging —are all prerequisites for status and instant gratification in the book world. With constant author feeds and group numbers —page reads, algorithms, and insights, terminology becomes a vast, mindless chasm.

To be the best, the biggest, top-ranked, and visible, you have to be willing to decimate anyone who threatens your position. This wasn't true of legitimate talent in the past—for the untrained, uninitiated, baby author, it's now the belief many hold fast. Worse than the social structure in high school, adults —we're talking twenty-year-olds— have become our cancel culture—entitled teens with limited skill sets.

An ingrained belief it's their right to take anything they see and pass it off as their own—from quotes to novels, photos to graphics, covers to content—everything is fair game. Everything is free if you can screenshot it online; just ask them. Why pay a creator for their work?

Self-imposed privilege, antisocial behavior, and zero moral fiber drive them. You'd not piss on one if they're on fire. You'd never associate with them in real life. You'd not want them in the safety of your home.

The morals most humans inherit from birth appear absent in the new breed of author. They're sofa surfing, pajama warriors, bulldozing and annihilating anything in their path.

This monumental rise equates to fast release, make bank, and run. Desperate authors and personal assistants—a bottomless pit of information, temptation, and a cesspool of corruption. Apex predators, with a limited life expectancy.

The ability to hide behind a keyboard and reinvent is mind-blowing. From creating pen names, fan bases, blogs, and private boost groups–the control they believe they hold is terrifying. No talent's required, in a sea of alias' and duplicates—often triplicates. The only qualification is the ability to read, review and promote on multiple platforms.

We permit ourselves to be manipulated, filling an empty corner of our soul. Wanted, needed, appreciated; it's human nature after all. Invited—included in a small way—to an exclusive organization is an adrenaline rush. I've experienced it–it's like no other.

The negative aspect of a beautiful craft now far outweighs the positive.

You may ask, are there still authors worthy of support, of devoted followers? Authors who share our love of the written word, fine-tuning their craft, not the bottom dollar. Ones who'd never steal from others, or manipulate the system rankings, or reviews—ruining it for all who follow. Do any remain with work ethics ingrained?

In my case, as a reader, I am who I am. No filters, no fake accounts. Gullible in the belief a remnant—a tiny sliver of good —hides in this world, and our society. Am I naïve to pray there are still decent human beings remaining post covid? The last vestige of wonder and magic in the publishing world was ripped away then. All that's left is a jagged, seeping, necrotic wound for most committed readers.

In hindsight, would I do this again, recognizing the corruption firsthand? Would I step into the lion's den, knowing they'll eat up many? So few will survive if we stay silent.

Or, do I disappear into the shadows as they pray I, and many others will—or do we take a final stand?

It's the million-dollar question.

They manipulate the masses. They influence a book release.

They make or break an author. A vicious shell game shuffles the day's chosen, attention-seeking book whore—The Smut Mafia.

Chapter One

Kat

Past

11:35 am Tuesday 2nd August.

"Kat? Are you home? Your gourmet meal's arrived." Sara's voice echoes from the empty atrium of my father's home. I hear the rustle of paper bags, as she moves into the kitchen with groceries.

Jotting down my last thoughts, keystrokes click on my typewriter-style keyboard, comforting me in their familiarity. I race to add another few random thoughts kicking around in my skull.

Journal note:
Readers remember the vermin, pure and simple. I'd liken them to roof rats, bastards are damn hard to get rid of. Cockroaches are a better analogy. They're able to survive a nuclear holocaust, determined little bastards. Bottom feeding groups return with a vengeance, breeding the next mutant generation, unhindered.

"Sorry, I was on a roll. I had to get this down before it disappeared into the abyss." I chuckle at my joke. The dark depths of my hard drive consume thousands of words daily, never to see the light.

"You're going through with this then, Kat? You're finally going to publish?" Sara's excitement is almost contagious.

"Nope. It's for my benefit." If I could suppress the acrid taste in my mouth, contemplating going live, I'd take the risk.

Pursing her lips, an all too familiar scenario's about to play out. "What's the point then? It's written, what's the point if you keep polishing it? They're only going to return strengthened and immune to repercussions. Why leave them standing? How many more will suffer at their hands?"

"One, it's cathartic? Two, it's not my responsibility to sacrifice myself for others who are ignorant of the inner workings. Most people read for pure pleasure, they've no idea how indie functions. Why spoil it for someone else? Brutally shoving authors from pedestals, to show they're mere mortals achieves nothing. One day—one day I'll grow a set and take the plunge, not right now."

"And when you do? What's it going to resemble? A fluffy unicorn glitter fest, or hell and brimstone?"

My staunchest ally, Sara's always ready to rumble. If she hadn't picked me back up from the depths of a dark hole after Dale and the chat drama, I don't know where I would be.

"Napalm, hellfire, and big fucking boots—I'll throw it all at them. No one will see it coming and I'll sleep again at night."

"I'll bring the marshmallows and vodka for the bonfire, hon."

"It's a date, Sara."

"Don't leave it too long Kat. We love you. We want you back in the land of the living."

Sara's reassurance warms my heart, and adds to my resolve to make this right.

Chapter Two

Kat

Past

6:40 pm Friday 5th August.

My lunch date with Sara stuck with me all week, reliving the past I'd buried. Conversations played on repeat, living rent-free in my head, taking up more space each hour. The what ifs, circling like birds of prey, waiting to pick bones clean the moment I closed my eyes.

Nestled with hot cocoa in my favorite recliner, defying the summer heat, I grab my phone and hit her number.

"Hey, hon. I know this is short notice, but are you up for a few drinks? Our little discussion kept me awake, I'd love to run something by you."

An excited squeal rings in my ear. "Does this mean?"

"Working on it. I'll order pizza."

"You go, girl! I'll pick up Zan on the way. We'll see you in an hour."

Cutting off the call, sweat breaks on my forehead. Shaking, I drop my phone to the table, dragging in air, and run my fingers along my inked wrist. Not committing to this madness once and for all, hasn't eased the pain in my chest every time I remember Evie. She loved this community with her all, but where did it leave her in the end?

Stuffed with pepperoni pizza, I grab the tubs of ice cream to finish off our amazingly satisfying meal.

"Vanilla's mine." Sara snatches the proffered spoon, hugging hers tightly.

"I don't understand how you can stomach vanilla, Sara." I cringe at the memory it invokes.

"At least it's pure vanilla, not the fake crap," Zan mutters around a mouthful of creamy butterscotch goodness.

"Be thankful for sweet mercies. At least the extract is macerated vanilla bean paste in alcohol."

"*Exactly*. Alcohol and ice cream are a must." Sara's cheerful voice is muffled by her spoon, balanced precariously between her lips.

"See, Zan knows it's the vanilla flavor I'm on about. The cheaper alternative, essence—do you know where it comes from?" I cringe at the memory of my first search as a kid on this one. "It comes from the anal glands of beavers. How the fuck anyone considers this essential to baking, or who thought beaver ass was a good idea, I'll never understand."

Zan dry reaches, as Sara breaks into fits of laughter, tears streaming down her face. "This is why we love you, Kat. Random dinner conversation we don't need."

Eyeing off the folder between us, Zan shuffles forward,

waving her ice cream-coated spoon like a maestro. "Time to fill us in on your impromptu get-together?"

"Ladies, my detailed notes so far." Tipping back the last of my merlot, I eye the suspiciously empty glass.

"Cenosillicaphobia," Sara groans, waving hers in unison. "Word of the day. A drinker's fear of an empty glass."

"Next one's on me." Zan bounces into the kitchen, her dark dreads hitting her ass. Dropping back down beside me, bottle in hand, she refills my drink. Sliding her fingers down my new ink, her melancholy voice hits hard. "I know it's corny, I need this one too." She circles the feathers falling from a broken heart—dark, shaded barbed wire splits it dead center; entwined with *Vive ut vivas*, ending in a soft watercolor, blue quill. The mix of old and new styles, a day I'll never forget. "Evie would have loved this, babe. You did well."

One of the last anchors in my life, Evie's loss will live with me forever, now it's indelibly inked into my skin.

Sara's sad smile, a reflection of her missing twin, reminds me of how much we all suffered. She bumps her glass to mine, "Cheers. Where are we then?"

"Step one, current research on how to publish. I've looked at the benefits of an agent versus a direct marketing spiel to a publishing house. A publisher won't let me in the door, let alone their foyer or front desk." I rattle off my first paragraph of information. Even the suggestion of putting myself out there terrifies me.

"Always negative. Give me a sec." Zan scrolls through her phone. "Agents. Hmm, so many choices. What if I could get you in the door with a publisher?" Her pause for effect tickles my odd sense of humor, and I choke on my wine. "*Found it.* How's this sound? Mid-sized has a few big names under its umbrella. Ooh, hot head shot. This one's cover model ready." Flashing the screen our way, Zan cackles with glee. "I met him at a cause fundraiser last Spring. Up and coming, used to be a… let me check." Another quick scan over her expansive notes. I swear her life story's contained in her phone.

"How many are you up to now, Zan? She's collecting boy toys, real live Ken dolls, by the way," Sara slurs, hiccuping, as she leans into my left shoulder. Wrapped up with my girls, post pizza binge, wine on hand, death by carbs—this is my ultimate Friday night.

"Hmm, too many? I need to back this up again, I'm lost if my phone fails. Here he is. Ex-journalist. He's low ranked in the agency, he seemed honest in the sea of toy soldiers."

"What? Soldier. Pass. After Dale, I'm hardly going to work with one." The slightest suggestion of another military connection sets my stomach churning.

Sara, apparently reinvigorated, and no longer suffering from her inebriated state, joins Zan in stalking social media. "No, this one's the real deal. He saw action and didn't ride a desk. Breathe, Kat." Expelling a deep breath, I watch mesmerized as Sara scrolls, hunting her target. "See, September 2012. Damon Deverge received a medal for saving his interpreter's life. Took a bullet himself. I'd screw him," she groans, dramatically sinking into the sofa again.

Leaning into the photo, warm, soulful, whiskey-colored eyes drag my attention from Sara's chatter—pools of liquid bronze, lined with shadows, stare mournfully back at me. A well-muscled body, hidden by camo, dark hair disheveled, with a slight scruff on his jaw, *hot*.

A shoulder bump and giggle, Sara's knowing grin jump-starts my imagination. "So, he's ok?" She winks, and I can't help but join in on her light-hearted mood.

"Did you wink at me? This feels like high school all over again."

Zan collapses into giggles, nudging her phone toward me. "A pretty face is easier to work with if you know what I mean. I'll vouch for his credibility. He's a total gentleman and didn't even make it to first base on our date." Zan's notorious love 'em and leave 'em rotation meant this one was strictly in the safe zone.

"I'll think about it. Give me a day or two, I need to look into my options further."

Chapter Three

Kat

Past

Friday 12th August.

Now I understand why indie is easier. Agents' wish lists were publicly available via their portfolios. They outlined current tropes they were willing to consider submissions for. After a week wasted throwing out proposal letters, I relented and followed the bio link Zan sent me. Working back from the publisher's home page, I compiled my to-do list.

The list grew rapidly as I ticked off each requirement.

- Query letters and paper manuscripts—the old-school preferred methods.
- Digital submission is preferred by other houses, not by J.D.
- Proposal.
- Edited or unedited? Easy choice. I'm sending it edited, who wants to read rough notes?
- Agent - submit to the agent with open submissions for the genre *only*!

- Reiterate, *only* query the agent if they're listing the genre and offer active openings.
- Film options and foreign rights. Yeah, right. I wish but noted the house and its agents were familiar with them.
- Terms - fifteen to twenty percent commission depending on the market location.

Literary agents with experience in editing, film, and tv.

Zan was spot on with this connection for once. They appear to be a good fit, so what do I have to lose? What's another rejection in a life already inundated with them? My words are out there already, through no fault of my own, so I have nothing to lose.

Loading up a few chapters, the plot outline, and a cover letter, I hit send before I can change my mind. I've already secreted hard copies as a backup to Zan. Heaven forbid something crashes, or I lose my marbles and delete my work again.

Fingers crossed my over-eager email encourages someone in Mr. Deverge's office to open the envelope Zan delivers.

*Introductory chapter/outline, submitted
to J.D. Publishing LLC.*

Why do we read?

Those first words—the first seven minutes—are reminiscent of a warm hug, delving into a story you pray you'll love.

Those first seven minutes make or break a book.

If words don't grab us within the first few pages, the author knows we'll throw their book on top of a did not finish pile. The sea of books flooding retailers is never ending, without a hook, readers move on to the next on offer.

Those first seven minutes, our brains are inundated with

subliminal messages and imagery. We're assured a book is fantastic. It's dark, smutty, spicy, amazing—full of twists and turns—as reviewers warn us, in their generic, hyped reviews. So, we one-click and it sits unread forever on a device, or we binge read on release, to fit in with the in-crowd.

Those first seven minutes make or break a book.

Blogger posts, promo, propaganda—all cleverly designed to convince readers they're failures if they don't buy and love the latest release—the chart-topper, the best seller. Those impressions dig deep into a reader's psyche, asking if they're good enough, should they ever doubt the hype. Doubt the online friends they've never met. Doubt strangers whose one aim is to push.

So, you want to publish your book?

Welcome to our how-to guide for best-selling cliterature. Please take this comedic portrayal of publishing with a pinch of salt. If there was any truth to it, imagine the Tower of Babel falling—the results would destroy our bookish world as we know it. If we contemplate the secrets imagined within are remotely plausible it's a disservice to those who create for the pure love of words—seen but never read. Complexities and drama aside, ask yourself this–is it possible?

Let's begin indie 101, and how to reach those stars.

You've watched the latest made-for-TV series or blockbuster movie. You came up with the perfect twist and reimagined ending. Our hero needed his ever after, the heroine needed saving, and you threw yourself in, full steam ahead.

Words flew onto the pages—action, adventure, fantastic porn-level sex scenes, and your friends loved it! Cliches abound. Catch phrases, and brand names were thrown   in, and you stayed true to your country of origin. You wrote about a graphic event in the US or an amazing rescue mission in the Amazon.

Sounds simple, doesn't it? You dive into the cover market, and grab a bargain pre-made, it feels familiar, but heck, aren't they all? Source an online editor, they'll send your manuscript back at an exorbitant fee per word. Next, someone turns those words into a retail-friendly file. It is formatted for you, click upload, and you have self-published on major ebook sites. Congratulations, you are now a published author!

But where are your sales, page reads, and income return? You've outlaid thousands. It looks pretty, your friends loved it. Where did you go wrong?

Let's face facts, publishing's a process of fine-tuning, research, and hours upon hours of editing—often thousands for a series, and it is not an easy task. Who's to say anyone will ever find this little piece hidden away in the swamp of independent books?

Success, or failure, is contingent on algorithms, far beyond our comprehension. The dissent amongst small indie authors—their worth measured against others—is mind-blowing. Hard work, or time served, is no longer ingrained in an upcoming protege. Instant fame, fortune, and fan base are demanded by the majority. Bloggers become authors, with well-established social media followers. Very little skill set—zero formal training—flooded the market in recent years. These are the new creators overloading the book charts. Imposter syndrome is real. Algorithms make or break an author, as does word of mouth.

Questions arise when it's taken too far. What are we left with in the ashes of discontent?

In my case, each breath, each thought, and each step were choreographed per a schedule. Color outside the lines—the hand of the Smut Mafia, slapped me back down hard.

I was suffocating, drowning in plain sight, inch by devastating inch. Most claim drowning is peaceful. I'll deny it—every second was excruciating. Death welcomed me with open arms, the living dragged me back into their fold— gnarled fingers dug deep into my skull.

Dramatic? No. To this day I can still feel their talons grazing my

In amongst the beauty of creation, entwined in words we adore, lurks a hidden evil. Pandora's box, if you wish. A world of subterfuge, pyramid schemes, pirated books, theft of works—the Smut Mafia. This is their story.

Sleep eluded me. By six am, I'd already showered and picked up the week's worth of housework and laundry I had conveniently avoided. I prayed my email to the J.D. Publishing account went to spam, or disappeared into cyberspace. Unsend was not an option.

My phone pinged a little after six pm. A day debating the insanity that gripped me clicking send, and overthinking scenarios of rejection, I'd deleted my email app as a means of avoidance. Reluctantly I reinstalled it so I could communicate with my banking clients, the ones who paid my bills working from home.

I scrambled to check my email, floored to open up Damon's correspondence.

Dear Ms. Campbell,

I acknowledge the manuscript submission of your fiction novel, PuSh, and propose a meeting with you at your earliest convenience. I'd enjoy discussing the below points, along with a provisional offer.

The agent-author relationship is imperative to promote our clients from the first draft to the published manuscript; we have the capabilities to consider optioning your work and take further steps with other publishing mediums.

We pride ourselves on establishing a sound working relationship with our clients.

While we are a mid-sized house, we offer hands-on contact, through all aspects of the publishing process, within the confines of our business.

Our authors aren't just a number, they're family.

I'm here to help grow your career, and most importantly, to ensure you succeed. I'll assist in polishing the manuscript, act as a sounding board, and feed your muse if required.

I'll ensure you receive the highest possible advance on your work and find a team member who fits your vision; one willing to work for you, not treat you as a product. Someone who sees the potential in your words, and is willing to invest quality time, and money, in making your dreams come true.

I look forward to your response and hope we may meet at a time convenient to you very soon.

Sincerely,

Damon Deverge
J.D. Publishing

Dear Ms. Campbell,

I acknowledge the manuscript submission of your fiction novel, PuSh, and propose a meeting with you at your earliest convenience. I'd enjoy discussing the below points, along with a provisional offer.

The agent-author relationship is imperative to promote our clients from the first draft to the published manuscript; we have the capabilities to consider optioning your work and take further steps with other publishing mediums.

We pride ourselves on establishing a sound working relationship with our clients.

While we are a mid-sized house, we offer hands-on contact, through all aspects of the publishing process, within the confines of our business.

Our authors aren't just a number, they're family.

I'm here to help grow your career, and most importantly, to ensure you succeed. I'll assist in polishing the manuscript, act as a sounding board, and feed your muse if required.

I'll ensure you receive the highest possible advance on your work and find a team member who fits your vision; one willing to work for you, not treat you as a product. Someone who sees the potential in your words, and is willing to invest quality time and money in making your dreams come true.

I look forward to your response and hope we may meet at a time convenient to you very soon.

Sincerely,

D Deverge
Damon Deverge
J.D. Publishing

Holy crap, what have I done? There's no taking it back now.

Chapter Four

Damon

Present
Dave's Bar & Grill, 12:15 pm Friday, August 19.

Sweet temptation.

The decrepit dimly lit bar reeked of stale cigarettes and beer. My shoes hit the tacky floor, popping with each step. Contemplating the potential biohazard I've stepped in, my OCD ramps. Imagining disgusting microbes and viruses in the slurry, and inhaling secondhand smoke–is the reason I rarely set foot outside of the office for client meetings.

The heat hits me in stifling waves, the venue's lack of air conditioning evident. I'm sweating in my button-down and vest–the signature persona I've assumed as my professional attire. As much as I'd like to turn tail and run, I need this. I need a novel to propel me into the big leagues at J.D. Publishing. The premise and plot outline, while only a few chapters, were fascinating. Discovering the submission in a slew of ever-hopeful, persistent, would-be-authors manuscripts, was invigorating.

Our open slot policy meant we needed to consider every option presented. This one, hell, she could sell ice to Eskimos with her diatribe.

The old me—the scavenging journalist, arose from the ashes igniting something I'd thought long gone. The fervor in so few words left me begging for sustenance. Make or break, my intuition has never failed me. This is the big one. There's a best-seller written all over it.

With reticence, I seat myself on the worn red polyester seat. As instructed, I'd found the dark nook beside a plastic potted palm tree, segregated from the main bar. The specifics of our meeting were a tad bizarre; cloak and dagger were an understatement.

The gum-chewing waitress places a beer mat down and pours water into an ice-filled glass beside me. "What can I get you?" With the gentle tap-tap of a stylus against her digital pad, she waits for my order.

"Waiting for a friend, thanks, June." Her name badge pinned precariously on her left, with a *have a nice day* smiley face, is a little too much.

Jaded eyes peer from an overly made-up face. Outdated makeup reminds me of a fifties billboard sign. Green eyeshadow compliments the logo on her shirt. Her black wingtips finish an exaggerated look, but there's an allure beneath the caked-on mess.

"Give me a yell when you're ready, hon," a nod, and she moves on to the next high-top. I watch her pace through the tables; clichéd, stonewashed black denim, clings to her Rubenesque figure, as she totters on high, red heels. She greets the next table, her friendly demeanor impervious to the lewd jokes thrown her way. Taking their order, she pushes the stylus behind her ear, glances back at me, and I respond with a negative grin.

Re-checking my phone, my potential client is late—fifteen

minutes exactly. It doesn't bode well for my best-seller dream. I scroll through emails, lost in thought, and miss the lithe figure slide into the seat opposite.

"Do you know the title of the world's best-selling book? Written by the hand-of-man, purported to be words whispered by a higher being?" Dulcet tones–sex on a stick, was once the phrase coined in movies—glide over my ears.

"Hi, let me introduce…" a raised hand stills my response. Charm-filled bangles, rattle and slide down from her fragile wrist to her elbow.

"The second highest published book was delivered in chapters by a teenager, on a free platform. A fictionalized lifestyle became not only a best-seller, but a multi-billion dollar movie franchise." Her breathy laugh leaves me grinning. I'm immediately captivated by her wit and no-nonsense attitude. "I'm K… I'm Evie, by the way."

Perfect, manicured, blood-red nails slide against dark shades. Removing them, I realize Evie's older than I thought. Honey blonde hair, no longer held back by the frames, falls across her cheek. I'm mesmerized by the finger twirling the end of a lock, tucking it back behind her delicate ear. Tiny crystal books hang from gold hoops, catching her hair. The bangles tinkle, sliding back down, as she drops her hand. My eyes follow the delicate shaded calligraphic font wrapped around her forearm. Ending in a blue quill at her wrist, I can't catch the first half obscured by her sleeve. The ink looks fresh, the skin pink-tinged along the edge. My first impression is one of confusion. The eclectic image she presents contradicts her no-nonsense story—she recognizes my interest immediately.

Creases line her eyes, and light dances within. A cheeky smile pops from plump, ruby-glossed lips. Pearls—who still wears pearls? —drape her neck, their luster picked up by the flickering downlights. The black lace trim of her bra peeks from beneath a retro v-neck band t-shirt. Nothing about her odd ensemble fits the image I'd formed following her subterfuge.

"So, you're interested in publishing my nefarious and scandalous little tale, hmm?" Sultry, hinting at well-kept secrets, her voice tempts me further. Drawn to her and the promise of illicit stories, I lean in closer.

"Yes, ma'am. We'd enjoy discussing options further. A little backstory would go a long way to cementing the deal and helping pick the team." Swiping my phone screen, I lay it face up between us, my app ready to record. "May I?"

With a flash of bright white teeth, Evie bites and plays with her bottom lip. With an almost imperceptible nod, I push to record.

*Damon Deverge, and Evie Campbell, 12:45
pm Monday, April 22, 2022.*

"Nice to meet you, Evie. I love what I've read so far. Tell me, how did something seemingly innocuous become mind-blowing and complicated? For all intent and purpose, you appear to be normal—not politically correct, I know. You're intelligent, clued in, you're not a kid stepping out alone for the first time. How did reading a simple romance book twist upon itself so deviously? The story sounds reminiscent of a spy thriller."

Evie taps the side of her nose, a smirk covers her lips and I'm fascinated to hear more. "Thanks for meeting with me, Damon. I guess it's very much a suspense plot, in a non-fiction trope. How do I put this? I'm not melodramatic. The simplest answer is everyone stole a piece of my soul." Her shoulders shrug, I can envision cogs in her mind ticking over as she navigates the labyrinth her life became. "Did you ever play seven minutes in heaven?"

With a twinkle in her eyes and a cheesy grin, I can picture this woman as a teen, diving into a closet. She may not be a ringleader, but others willingly followed her. There's an... attraction isn't the term. Something glimmers below the surface. Hints of light and dark draw me to her—she's an enigma.

"Sure. A few times." Heat creeps up my cheeks. "I was the pimply-faced teen they dared others to make out with. I wasn't a catch." My expertise was limited then, as it is now. But now, my abstinence is by choice. The tangent she's heading appears strange, but I'll play along.

"You played, right? Delved into the dim light and allowed another to guide you?"

"It was a game—peer pressure. Of course, I played."

"Think bigger. On a grander scale, with a golden ticket waiting at the end." Fingers reach for the empty water glass, shaking, nails tap the side.

"Another? Coffee?" Her hand stills and the nervous tremor abates. I push further into her personal space, and trace lines down the wood grain toward her. My fingertip wipes condensation droplets as I go.

"Coffee. Great. Sorry, bad habit." Pulling into herself, nails digging into her palm, Evie's knuckles whiten.

Wanting to distract her actions, inexplicably, I'm hit by the need to protect her. My fingers slide closer, infiltrating her comfort zone.

She leans back from the table, hands face down, unflinching.

Challenge accepted.

"Why now? Based on the few chapters you've submitted this is nothing new, it's a long-term issue. What's pushed you to come forward, to publish?"

"Because I have nothing left to lose. Someone who paid attention—with an almost photographic memory—is detrimental to the status quo. Dangerous. We lost someone close to us."

"I'm sorry for your loss." I kick myself at the rote platitude. "Time to clear the air, or burn it all down sums you up then?" I watch a spark of fire ignite in her eyes. A fervor drives her—missing in the book community for far too long. Corrupted by everyone out for themselves, it's refreshing to see such passion.

"History has taught us one thing in literature–classics stand tall and remain revered. So, pray tell me, how does swill make it to the top, day in, day out? Dismally elocuted words, appallingly constructed plots—readers overlook editing, tense, and grammar. How do they achieve greatness?"

The intelligent conversation wrapped up in a gorgeous package, jolts my cock to life.

"Coming from a traditional aspect, they wouldn't achieve the fame or infamy, many appear to have gained. Most are shut down before entering our doors. Readers at least expect a standard in the printed word."

"Hmm, exactly. At which point will the masses wake up and question what's force-fed and read the book content?"

Evie's long exhale, eases my fear she wouldn't pull this off and weather the coming storm. She might not look it, but she's courageous—the tenacity to come this far speaks volumes for her dedication.

Without skipping a beat, she proceeds. "There's no longer a clear black and white definition on the page. It's now a murky, pungent, noxious mire. I want to admire authors again. Read without smudged glasses or cynicism, second-guessing whose work it is. I need to believe something good endured, after all the evil I've witnessed."

Fifteen minutes in her company, I've only glanced briefly below the cracked surface. I'm confident she's talented enough to execute the plot outlined to its full potential. If her zeal is anything to go by, there's ass-kicking on the agenda.

Her eyes wander, a red nail pointing to my phone, I cease recording. With a hum of approval, the intensity emanating from her hits me. Evie's demeanor alters, clearly pleased to be in charge.

I slide the contract and offer toward her. "Time for you to sign on the dotted line, Kat. You may leave your pen name at the door in the future. It's time to clean house."

Glancing at the neatly typed contract, with a nod and a grin, it disappears into her purse. "Where do we begin?"

Chapter Five

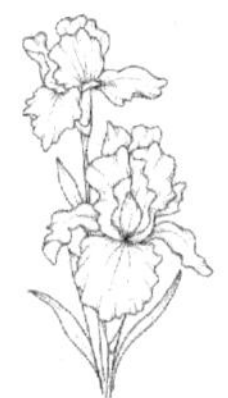

Kat

Past: Kat's journal

Social media is addictive. I mistakenly believed I'd found my safe place during a tumultuous time in my life, amongst like-minded people. They offered no judgment or shame. A simple gathering of readers and authors, all on an equal footing as human beings.

Those who read, won't steal books, and those who can write, know better–or so I thought.

In hindsight, we were never equal. In hindsight–they were soul-sucking demons who drained every single drop of time and energy, with no remorse.

Perhaps it's best to go back to where it all went wrong...If only we could turn back time.

K&E's_book_smut chat. 10:40 am Tuesday, January 2nd.

Evie: Babe, morning check-in. Rant on JJ's author page. Oh my fucking god. Doesn't she understand how unprofessional it is?

Kat: Hey lovely, how was your date? Yeah, I read it first thing. Funnier still, Aria forgot which account she'd signed into and replied under her author name. Teach her to run five lol.

Evie: Insert eye roll. Pretty veneer, with the personality of a rock, won't be a second date any time soon? Aria? She's so sweet. I missed it. Did you screenshot the post?

Kat: Of course. They believe readers are naïve and ignore their bitch sessions. Their unsolicited opinions on reviewers being trolls—they need to grow up and develop a business plan. Don't they remember they were readers once, thinking they could do better?

Evie: Reba's all over social media bagging low ball reviewer ratings.

Kat: Not fucking hard to edit. Her arc team ignores typos and grammar, as instructed. Her readers purchasing the novel won't. They all need to tighten up. Don't ask for book reviews and duck when shit hits the fan.

Evie: My point exactly! I'm all for supporting a debut, but an established author churning out crap every release—it's embarrassing.

Kat: Mandatory new rules on Cash's signups. Must rate on release, within 24 hours. Now we're negative Nancy's, or trolls, if it's not a four or above.

Evie: Nope. Pass. Fuck that shit. I'm not bending over and taking it anymore. The first time, you might be nice and overlook or forgive issues. Every release, publishing someone else's old plot and recycling characters? Pass. It looks contrived, rating high, when it's an upper primary grade writing quality at best.

Kat: You realize they'll hit you hard if you're not placating Cash, right?

Evie: What? It's a novel. Are they going to hire a hitman and take someone out over reviews? If their plots weren't so full of drama and over-the-top sham mafia, I'd believe the threat.

Kat: It's only a book. I'm out, I know better than to open my mouth.

Evie: Block the bitches and step away.

Kat: Remember your next recommendation better be a good one. You owe me for this signup slump and bullshit drama.

Evie: On it already. I'll find us something to bite into. You'll see. Pinky promise xx

Evie

Adamant she would not let Kat down again with another dead end lead, Evie fed words to an A.I. chat bot. The only worth she had was the quality of words Kat could produce with little effort. In the back of her mind, she knew it was wrong, but entry, and ultimate acceptance, came at a price.

"Now let's rework the pesky copyright page. Don't wanna get caught claiming it's original content, right?"

All rights snagged. I own this fictional mess. No copying, stashing, or slinging it digitally—now or in some dystopian future—without my scribbled okay. Snip quotes for reviews? Fine.

A.I. trainers: Hands off—this ain't your data chow.

Pure fiction, folks. Names, spots, folks, and drama? All from my twisted brain. Real-world nods? Fake as a three-dollar bill; trademarks snuck in without a wink or nod from owners.

Any mirror to real peeps, groups, or chaos? Total fluke.

Big library-only gig; no sneaks elsewhere or ARC handouts. Bootlegged copy? Torch it and bow to my genius. No reselling or passing around, baby.

Evie laughed at her own twisted take on Kat's words. It actually worked. "I have a better idea, what about this?" She continued to mutter to herself and blend another's prose.

This is a snarky spoof of indie publishing's promo clown show. It's not real, and far from a tutorial—there are twists galore.

Triggers: Cyber-bullies, mind-melts, off-page self-sabotage. No real cheating (book hunks don't count). Slow-burn dual POV with timeline flips. Hate time-jumps? Bail now.

Newbies gobble social scraps, skip actual reads. If they cracked books, we wouldn't be in this mess. Readers? Sharp cookies—underestimate at them your peril.

She continued to move words around, caught up in the game. "Now I understand why this is so addictive." Her pencil raced across the lightly lined red book, secure in the knowledge the source was original.

Unseen souls: We're watching.
My crew: You know the deal—this one's yours.
Hate-stirring? Karma's a bitch.

Desperation gripped her. She was never going to let Kat down again. This time she had something perfect to offer the team as she brought up the chat window.

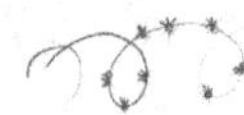

Private chat, Dee Dark

Evie: I have the perfect example of a rework for you, Dee. Check out this blurb.

What if everything you've—
Bought. Devoured. Flaunted.
In the last three years was,
Phony. Repurposed. Poisoned.
Still ready to smash that promo button and share ill gotten gains?
Did you eyeball the guts and scour ripped plots and lines first?
We sure as hell did.
Strap in—there's an 8 second ride ahead.
Armor up those big-girl undies; mess incoming...now.
Indie publishing, meet your mirror.
#smutmafiagate beckons.

Evie: Then I kind of played with the first chapter from Kat's journal.

The great heist—outline/notes, brain farts.

Romancelandia is Indie pub's 'best'? Ha.

The book crowd are all day suckers, bonded by ink, dodging daily dreck in dog-eared tomes.

Stories ancient as dirt swamp romance addicts, stoking feels. They teleport us, living large through strangers' scripts—craving nods, hugs, and love, via imaginary studs.

Reading=escape pod, cozy club, soul glue—blanket for bliss or blues. We hoard and hoard our smut.

The Indie game is a dream gig for paupers or princes. Authors juggle edits, bucks, covers, shills. Predators fleece noobs with junk services; saints guide gratis. Elite promo outfits? Picky or bust—scarred from ancient 'gates.'

Knowledge is power until one provides a tiny venomous sliver. Boom! Acid meltdown, worse than Chornobyl—they devour vibes with spite.

Readers catch that echo.

Outsider view: You're all raccoon-shit bonkers. No sane folk vibes here. Elite push only hijacked porn plots.

The new Author avalanche, amid a plague of panic, bred bedlam. Venom spewed; secrets teased, then squashed like rotten tomatoes. Shields on and offline, hide maniacal schemes.

D.D.: I love the racoon-shit bonkers, but you're trying too hard.

Dee eagerly reread the chapter. A fresh take might work to their advantage, dependent of course on what Evie wanted.

D.D.: You know she'll hunt you down if she works out you nicked this, right?

Evie: She loves me, so no. I'm all she has, even if it is noticed. Please be discreet and add it somewhere quietly.

The chat screen ceased moving, as Evie waited for a golden ticket.

Evie: Is it good enough? I can do better, if you give me a chance. *We* can do better.

D.D.: I'll do you a favor, don't tell the others, right?

Evie: Of course I won't, cross my heart.

D.D.: Slide into my docs and drop these in then. You have hidden skills, my little mouse.

Evie: Thank's Dee. Just one thing. You promised if I bought you something good, you'd invite Kat too.

D.D.: Sure thing. We can always use an extra blogger.

Evie: Thank you so much!!! You're my hero!!! You won't regret this.

Chapter Six

Kat

Present

7:45 am Thursday, 8th September 2022.

The elemental pull of a harvest moon sparked creativity I'd lost many years ago.

My batteries recharged, like the crystals lining the picture window frame, brought hope to my dark heart. Perhaps Damon was right, I needed a new outlook. A wake-up call if you must. Roll on mid-life crisis.

Eyeing my phone charging, I switch to work mode. No social media today, it impairs my thought process. I'm too old for this shit, let the kids play. My muse calls, his voice screaming in my ear, desperate to be heard…It's been a snowball ride in hell and plagiarism is the minuscule tip exposed in a mountain of shit. I need to compile my notes, go over them again, and return the edited manuscript update to Damon.

The smell of coffee percolating in the machine drifts from my kitchen. The ping of my alarm announces it's a new day, there's no time to waste.

I'm ready to claim my place at the table and defy the odds. There may be three million books published daily this month, I'm adamant I'll add mine to the list.

Lost in thought, a slow, melodic beat, plays in the background. The scratch of the stylus on the old record player adds to the ambiance. My playlist is limited to eighties and nineties remixes, depending on my mood. Lyrics draw memories my subconscious doesn't want to reveal. My muse says otherwise–it's time.

A key rattles my front door, Damon shoulders it open, arms full, taking in the kitchen disaster behind me. Working at the table allows for ready access to caffeine and snacks. It is glaringly obvious by the mess they are frequent.

Resembling tornado alley, takeout boxes line every free space, and the sink overflows with dishes. Wrinkling his nose, he drops the grocery bags against the fridge.

"Housekeeping quit, or was the frat party moved here?" he jests.

I inhale his tantalizing aftershave, the scent of leather, notes of cedar, and a spicy tone I can't quite place. "I'm working. I'd have dug deep and done a trash run if I'd known you were coming." I shuffle my bare feet, and the blackened nail of my big toe protrudes from my unicorn pajama pants.

"If your phone was on, you'd know it's Thursday, and brunch was on me, Kat."

"It's Wednesday. You're not due until tomorrow. Right? Did we move up the schedule?" Confusion laces my voice—we have rules and boundaries laid out—times we meet, updates, all on my terms. The house key was an emergency option. With no one else close by, kicking around alone now in my family home, it made sense to leave it in care with Damon.

"Where's your phone? Find it, I'll unload groceries and tackle this disaster zone."

Paper bags rustle behind me, grabbing an empty pizza box, I search for my damn phone. It was in my hand only moments ago.

"While you're at it, a shower won't go astray. You look like something the cat threw up." His chuckle echoes down the bare floors, enveloping me in warmth. It has been too long since I felt cared for.

"Anything else, your lordship?" My latent sense of humor spikes finally.

Damon

Cringing, my sinuses take offense, stale food and garbage line every surface. I need to juggle my time better and check in more frequently. I knew she was alone out here, but this isn't healthy.

"So, Kat. When was the last time you set foot outside? There has to be a week's worth of leftovers here." My question disappears down the empty hallway. I hear the sound of water running, as steam drifts from the open door. One point my way at least.

The first objective achieved, I discover garbage bags and haphazardly stuff everything I can reach into them. Wiping down the countertops, I assess the gourmet selection of deli meats, tapas, and biscotti I bought to tempt Kat.

"Hey, Kat? How about we try out the park down beside Lane? Fancy a picnic?"

Wet hair streams down her back, tired emerald eyes, peer out from bangs overdue for a trim. Elfen-like, in her lagenlook layers, barefoot, she props up the door frame.

"I guess so?"

"A little more enthusiasm, babe. It's warm out, I have coffee." Popping the lid, I wave my hand over the warm brew. Steam wafts, tempting cinnamon fills the room. "See, I remembered. Pumpkin spice season has arrived."

A warm, spring breeze lifts silky fine hair; her voice, melodic and pensive, buries itself in my gut.

Brunch and time away from the confines of my office, the first day I've played hooky in years, was worth it. The time spent working with Kat the past few months reminded me there's life outside of the safe world I've created.

Observing closely via our check-ins, Kat's appeared increasingly withdrawn. Today's date clicks, how could I forget?

"Have you heard from the boys?"

With a quick shake of her head, shadowed eyes greet mine. The spark I'm familiar with dimmed, as her divorce paperwork was finalized.

"I can't, Damon. I'm not going there today. No, I've not spoken with them. They're all off at school now, and Dale's restricted contact. He's upholding the custody agreement. It's in their best interest."

Her shoulders slump, but not before I catch a single tear sliding down her cheek. Standing up for a cause, inevitably broke her spirit and heart.

I reach out tentatively and wipe away the moisture. "Was it worth it Kat? Do you regret coming forward?"

"Not for a minute. Indie must change, we can't go on. Everyone's broken and disheartened." She picks absently at the tartan blanket beneath her.

My fingers slide down of their own accord, and lightly trace the tattoo below her elbow. "You promised to tell me her story one day."

Downturned eyes peer up at me. "You're already watching it unfold." She avoids eye contact, as I lean in closer to hear her muttered words. "You asked, was it worth it? Too little too late —but for Evie, I have to go through with it. Otherwise, what becomes of those pure, natural-born talents, hidden in the sludge if I give up now? What becomes of the Evies of this world?"

"What about the Kats?" Running my fingers along her pulse point, I feel her heart race.

"Evie will always be with me. It's their loss not having met and loved her the way I did. The world's a darker place without her fire lighting our way." Dragging her hand from mine, picking up her shoes, Kat hurriedly grabs her purse and keys. "Thanks for lunch and checking in on me, Damon."

"Give me a moment, I'll pack this up and walk you home."

A brisk shake of her loose mane, she's already shut me out. "No, I'm fine. I'll see you next Thursday, ok?"

I watch her wander barefoot across the manicured lawn, to the dilapidated home she hides in. Her mission's coming to a close with publication. I ponder the future and value of whistle-blowing all over again.

Chapter Seven

Damon

Present

13th October 2022, J.D. Publishing

Plastics, they're everywhere.

Our meetings switched to video chats over the past two months—Kat claimed she needed privacy to read over final edits. On the pretext of discussing audio options, I dragged her rather unwillingly into the office today. The words are there, her work is sound, J.D. and the team are pleased with the progress. We've auditioned a couple of narrators, the plan is to release both ebook, paperback, and audio, at once.

My concern, however, is with Kat's well-being. Hiding away in her father's mausoleum, cutting off those closest to her, her girls reached out. Their attempts to motivate her beyond video chats, to resume her life after Dale, failed. Sara sees similarities between Kat and Evie—providing a redacted history, Kat couldn't.

I've come to recognize this mood as her manic phase of work. The need to verbalize her thought process drives her body into frantic motion–witnessed many times via remote. Audio narration input is the perfect opportunity to touch base.

Manuscript in hand, Kat throws herself from the blue corner chaise in my office.

"I was suffocating. Drowning in plain sight, inch by devastating inch. Most claim drowning is peaceful. I'll deny it every second. It's excruciating. Death welcomed me with open arms. The living dragged me back into their fold with gnarled fingers dug deep into my skull. Each breath, each thought, each step choreographed per a schedule. Color outside the lines—the hand of the Smut Mafia, slapped you down hard. Dramatic? No. To this day, their talons still slice my body." Her face is now flushed, and the tension is palpable. "See, the beat's off on the sample, it lacks desperation–zero emotion, it sounded like every other audio file. You can't distinguish between authors if they're all read in the same monotonous tone. There's narration and then there's voice acting."

Her breath whooshes out, pausing her tirade. The printout lies crushed between her hands, balanced on the edge of my hardwood desk. "If you've listened to Aria's latest, you'll understand. But she's in the top ten with a blogger-driven piece of recycled crap."

Kat resumes pacing the small office space I've occupied for three years. Her crepe pants swish with every step; heels click as rounds fire–her built-up anger and frustration pour out. So much for our audition run-throughs.

"How are readers unable to see this? The book was released in 2018. It flopped, she replaced the cover three times, with multiple book tours. Unpublished, and *magically*, it reappears four years later as a best seller—*but* it's the same shit, different day."

She snaps her fingers, and another piece of the puzzle falls into place. "Pretty face, easy to market. It's all about the plastic people. Twenty-somethings with firsts. Zero life experience." The rosy glow on her cheeks–animated–Kat's excitement is contagious.

"Hell, you could sell these kids an old red cover, bodice-ripper romance, and they'll rave about it," her honeyed voice drawls. "The daily fight remains for talented authors to be read, while buried below a pile of steaming shit."

Too close to home, I stifle a snort. "I remember my grandmother perched beside her stash of monthly porn, as my mother referred to them. She'd settle in her favorite chair, an iced tea, and cookies beside her, *shoosh* anyone who walked in. Her reading time was sacred." The sentiment tied to those back issues brought fond memories. Books piled high in her reading space, at her happiest with her nose buried in treasured romance novels. I can still imagine the smell of aging books in her room, as I reminisce.

"Exactly! Quick reads, mass-marketed, sold at every newsagent or corner store. They were light reading, but hardly literature." Drawing in a harsh breath, she gears up for more. "The depressing point in this rant is that *plastic trash makes bank*. They recycle work from others. They play dirty, backed by minions with no idea of the agenda. Driven by greed, prizes, gift cards, and a fake signature on a sticker—loyalty is purchased for a few cents. Honest authors—façades steal from them daily—all in the name of money."

"How exactly do they find their target audience? Where do they source readers, willing to ignore rules and be complicit in what's ultimately a ruse?" Shaking her finger, I realize it's not so easy to unravel the tightly woven intricacies of her mind.

"Let's play a game." Breathy laughter erupts from her swanlike throat. Kat runs a finger seductively down her cleavage. The cadence of my heart skips a beat, taking off like a racehorse, eager for the finish line–straight down south to my pants.

"It's no longer about the craft or sharing talent with a world hungry for original entertainment. It's not about hope–or the glimmer of light–in their dismal existence, novels provide readers. It's about the bottom dollar—and they're lazy. There's zero skill or structure. Rambling word vomit wrapped in pretty photos bordering on pornography—dripping wet appendages, words encouraging sex toys by the bedside table." My not-so-subtle seat shift triggers a knowing smirk. Pointing at her reading app, a top one hundred screenshot, we swing in yet another direction. "Now, look at the top five authors and their latest releases."

"What exactly am I looking at? They're four and five-star reviews, over a thousand on a week-old book. So, Aria's a popular author."

"Look inside the preview. Tell me what you see."

I flick open the sample chapter. "Editor, cover designer, and author. A similar format in independently published books, imitating their traditionally released counterparts. Nothing untoward, standard front matter."

Kat chokes on a stifled laugh.

"What's so funny?"

"The indie use of the word editor cracks me up every time. Do their editors own a manual of style? Do you think the author does? If not, why not? I feel for those formally trained in the craft. They argue every edit with uneducated children not willing to submit, their names forever tied to dismally produced book pornography."

Thumping hands in front of me, her small frame shakes

my desk. The momentum's an achievement considering its sheer weight. "Look more closely. What's missing?"

Stunned at my initial oversight, it's glaringly obvious. "Copyright notice. Why the hell would an author not assert their right? Hmm, so it's odd, an error, hardly an epic conspiracy."

"Open the second book link I've provided."

I open the second link and download the sample chapters.

Kat waits for a beat, tapping her lip impatiently. "Do you see the pattern now? Any similarities?"

An average prologue greets me again, lacking originality. After a quick scan and comparison, I raise my eyebrow. "I see where you're going now. Coincidence, pure and simple. There's a limited market for covers, freelance editors, they'll cross paths."

Pushing back from my desk, the click of her heels echoes in my relatively empty office.

"Fine. I'll grant you a concession. The resource pool is shallow, and you'd possibly follow your peer's recommendations. But shouldn't the sheer number pushed by a single group raise eyebrows?" Her pacing resumes and her momentum builds again; I'm quickly drawn back into her orbit, watching her hips swing. "Now pull up the reviews again and compare the bloggers."

I switch between open windows on my iPad, scanning reviews on two books, less than thirty days post-release. With a four-point-three average rating, they're both impressive. No orange best seller banner, the sheer number of unverified astounds me. Comparing arc versus verified, it appears they've pushed excessive early reads to promote and play algorithms. The ploy achieved a ranking quickly but didn't hold it due to the required seven consecutive days at number one to earn a flag.

"Do you see it?"

A literal movie-style light bulb moment sparks. "You've got to be *fucking* kidding me. Now I understand where you're going with this. Clever girl. How the hell did you work this out?" My cognitive response is to screenshot page after page of reviews.

Pen in hand, I begin jotting notes and saving account profiles. I suspect this is the tip of a colossal mindfuck of an iceberg, hidden in plain sight.

"Readers are gullible. They're inclined to believe pretty shiny things, and not look below the surface. Bloggers hold multiple accounts. I'd estimate that those performing review services for author teams, on average, hold a minimum of five profiles. Do the math. Twenty reviewers equate to one hundred release day reviews." With a half smile and frown, she points at my notes. "Pay attention to replicated reviews. Technically, a published review is copyrighted. Identically posted, word for word should raise alarm bells." Kat is in her element now.

I realize I'm only beginning to scratch the surface of an extremely well-plotted scheme. "If a reader was discerning, sure. Most one click or jump into the provider to read for free, too scared to dispute whether a book is great or not. If their opinion differs vastly from the majority, they'll not put themselves in the firing line and leave a lower rating."

"I'm tired of seeing posts that books won't be torn apart as literature in ten years, just ignore errors, it's smut. They're dissecting them now, and they always will with the next generation of readers. No one's safe, considering political implications or societal changes. Why put yourself at risk? How many books can you name in the last five years put under the social media microscope?"

She's spot on with this. It's a daily social media scandal. Red flagging books via dubious reviews is greedy and sheer stupidity. "Too many. Between book burning and banning, I'd rather burn

Strez Whol, and her cultish wanna-be's promoting scandalous claims while drinking on social media. I detest the topic. Watch how hard indie authors push to see their new release banned as a marketing ploy. Categories aren't difficult, place them where they should be and don't attempt to manipulate tropes to deceive everyone. Romance has a happily ever after, killing off the main character, leaving a widow, nothing happy about it—does not compute." They've lost their way, it's one thing I'm certain of now.

Excitement bubbles, Kat's up and flipping through pages in a folder. "Here's another. Throwing poly into young adult tropes, adding multiple partners, and violence—it's the same scenario. It makes zero sense to risk a release. I've set up the fire pit many times over winter needing to rid my home of their manipulation. Notoriety and sales skyrocket when a book is banned. We're all guilty of diving on the bandwagon to support the poor abused author, unwittingly encouraging their exploits. I'm shocked by the weak structure and content in most, hardly ban-worthy. I'm assuming it's the only way they're successful with a release in some cases? It implies the reading audience isn't overly selective on quality and believes the hype, a book is taboo. Readers click the pre-orders, the book hits devices—throw in a few well-placed reports, and the book is banned. *Bang*, instant best seller." Face flushed, short of breath, she's glowing. I love she's this passionate about an issue others ignore, and wrongly assume is how it's done.

"An understatement if I've ever heard one. Knowledge is power, the few skirting the edges teeter towards acceptance that things won't ever change."

She mulls over my point for a moment. "Force change. Educate readers and help open their eyes to corruption. Marketing schemes aside, money exchanges hands for the written word, it's a product. Ripping someone off, when money is tight everywhere—readers hold the power to veto this behavior." Fixated on the view, Kat's disappearing back into her headspace.

"Teach them their actions have consequences." My modulated voice penetrates her racing mind, dragging her back to the present.

"Hold them accountable, even if I martyr myself? This can't continue feasibly. The system is beyond fractured now, no one can hold their finger in the dam any longer to stop the flood. A torrential downpour is coming."

"Time to drop your first book then, Kat. I hope you are ready."

Chapter Eight

Kat

Four years prior.

The serendipitous discovery of a new author, is reminiscent of finding a hidden treasure. The excitement of opening the first page—a witty dedication and an amazing prologue–pure magic.

For an avid bookworm, it is often the beginning of an emotional love affair with a writer.

As readers, we delve into their words, immersing ourselves in a stranger's creativity and commending them on their bravery. To self-publish, for most, is a hard-fought journey. The threat of potential failure, highs and lows, self-doubt, and broken dreams–are daunting. A new author wanders in a sea of millions of books for little reward. It is gratifying to say I wrote my story, I published, I am an author—it often ends there.

Authors, especially independent ones, must be the complete package. Hardworking wordsmiths, stressing over plots, performing extensive research and character development—creating worlds we're eager to meet.

Readers debate over book boyfriends. Connections with fictional characters, filling emotional requirements, and addiction equally. Characters climb through the pages, ensnaring our hearts.

Some books take months to write—for many, it takes years to fine-tune their manuscript and craft. They're the real deal–the ones worth following and investing your money in. The ones who repeatedly re-edit and update–ensuring the best reading experience for old and new readers alike.

The final step in publishing is being brave enough to one-click. To upload their precious words for the world to tear apart.

Free online platforms are a godsend. Anyone can produce and self-publish their novel now. Anyone can find a creative space to sell their product. The book world is no longer restricted; solely contracted to traditional publishing houses and stringent deadlines. It still remains the ultimate prize–to sign a traditional publishing contract–to seize the golden ticket.

Accolades piled on these talented writers are well-deserved. It's hard work with little reward. They run social media accounts on multiple platforms and pray they'll find a reader base who adores the words they've gifted the world. A piece of their heart shared—words desperately waiting to be devoured by readers—appreciative of their blood, sweat, and tears poured into the pages we read. Words honestly slaved over.

In amongst the beauty of creation, entwined in words we adore, lurks a hidden evil. Pandora's box, if you wish. A world of subterfuge, pyramid schemes, pirated books, theft of works—the world of the Smut Mafia. This is their story.

K&E's_book_smut chat. 9:32 am Monday, June 4.

Kat: Seriously @Evie? Another smut group invitation?

My fingers fly frantically over the old keyboard.

Kat: I'm topped out. I can't read another book with zero plot, pure word vomit.
Evie: This is it. I'm in. You're in too if you want.

My phone vibrates. I can feel Evie's excitement pulsating in our chat, thrumming along invisible threads of technology. I adore her verve de vie, but she's always into the latest shortcut to fame or get-rich scheme.

Kat: In what? It's another book group. Cheesy name, lol. You can't expect more from twenty year olds pushing book porn. Cliterature at its best.
Evie: Shut up and listen. This is it, the big game. Think top of the food chain. These girls are the street team for Dee Dark. Click the fucking link and see.

Knowing Evie, she'll blow up my phone until I accept the invite. Insert eye roll. As much as I love her, the constant need for recognition does my head in most days.

Kat: Done. Can I get back to my book now?
Evie: @Kat!!!

I can hear her whine through the keystrokes. Thank the Lord it's not FaceTime.

Evie: You need to *look*. Give Dee your details. They send out loads of free stuff, and she'll stuff your device immediately.

The dots continue to play across our chat screen.

Evie: Please don't mess this up for me. I need this, @Kat. You know I can't afford to keep my KU subscription going. Don't forget the free part. You'll never have to purchase a book again.

Yeah, right. Evie may be my best friend, but her taste is like comparing potato chips to filet mignon. I can't read another plot-hole-filled, overly dramatic piece of fluff. I need maturity with my smut. Attempting to convince us murderous privileged academy kids will be our future president and world leaders–there's a rehash–then there's outright plagiarism.

Kat: I can still choose, right? I can read one or two, maybe pick something interesting, obligation free?

Evie: Dee said to tell you no pressure. We're all family. She wants you to meet a few of their favorites and see who you enjoy. No strings, I promise. Sending you the link now. Dive in and complete your details.

An external document link pings my message thread. I know the site's dubious reputation for unsecured data well.

Kat: Seriously? Smut Mafia sounds like a porn channel. No strings? Fine, I'll fill it out. I need to head offline, the kids will be out of school soon.

Evie: Just make sure you complete it all. Dee's waiting on your device address. She'll send you a few arcs straight away.

Kat: Advanced reader copies? How?

Evie: You know, those competitions you keep entering to win early copies before release? They've watched our comments in groups for months.

Kat: Creepy much? So, they're stalking readers in groups? These girls, how are they hooking you up with unreleased books? It took Becca years to get onto an author's team.

Smiley faces roll across the chat window.

Evie: This is a favor, ok? Just keep it quiet. What happens in chat, stays in chat. You can't disclose who they are. Nobody knows who's in here. You'll die when you see the members.

Kat: Sounds like a fight club. So, stupid question, why's it a secret chat?

Evie: For good reason. The team only, you'll see. The bonuses, signed books, gift cards—it's unreal. The swag Bex received, fuck me. Hoodies, tumblers. She said one of the girls received an e-reader.

Kat: Jealous much? I believe you, @Evie. Look, gotta rush. The kids just walked in. I need to play mom until Dale gets home. The boys have baseball after four. I'll look at this as soon as they've left for practice. Love you, babe. Catch you later.

Evie: Love you more. Check in when you've set it up.

*** Message request - Dee Dark. If you reply, Dee Dark will also be able to call you. Accept / decline.

D.D.: Hon. Evie mentioned you're interested in joining the team.

Kat: Hi @Dee. How cool is this? Huge fan!!! So, team? I thought it was a chat group, a book club type of deal.

D.D.: Team's the wrong label I should remember. LOL. We're not a street team. Socials shut them down as false news. We're influencers, you know.

Kat: Influencers? Don't you need ten thousand followers or something?

D.D.: No. It's all about insights and post-like interactions now. As influencers, we tell readers what's popular. Who to read, weekly giveaways on our pages.

Kat: Sounds great, but my IG's only a few family pictures and books I love.

D.D.: It's why you're perfect for this. Stay-at-home mom. You pick up free books and share, letting others know how great they are. They relate to you and your family and realize it's ok to read man chest covers and spice.

Kat: So, this is all legit, right? Nothing illegal? The books you sent me, they're not new releases. Why do I need to share them?

D.D.: You're doing the author a huge favor. Once they hit higher review targets, their books become visible. Book tours are legit. We're doing a little free promo, nothing more.

Kat: Visible? In what way? I'm not great with reviews. Those professional bloggers with fancy websites and blogs, they're better options, aren't they?

D.D.: No, not always. We're helping our authors become visible. If they hit fifty reviews, their book is recommended when you search a category. Often clicking on an ebook, below are similar books suggested, theirs becomes one of them.

Kat: Make sense. It's a marketing step, right?

D.D.: Exactly. Ok. Who's your go-to person for a book? Whose recommendation do you trust, to suggest the next one you'll buy?

Kat: Evie? Heaven knows how many book clubs and groups I've joined based on her suggestion. My feed is flooded with daily deals and advertising, I can't keep up. I trust Evie knows what's current.

D.D.: Exactly. She's been doing this for a while. Did you love them? Buy the author's books?

Kat: No. Most were too in your face. Smut, come pouring down legs kind of deal. I'm over it. Shit, I'm thirty-five with three boys. My toys do a better job than Dale these days. A twenty-year-old author's idea of hot sex is cheesy high school crap.

D.D.: Ain't it the truth, hon. They hit the clit once a year if they're lucky. All you do is skim the sexy scenes, you're not required to read them. You'll love the authors in chat with us. You get to read chapters early and have a little input into their work. It's fun and free, *and* they send out gift cards and books on release. Win, win.

Kat: Thanks. I think.

D.D.: You'll love it, don't stress. I rarely send random friend requests. My page is private. The same goes for my socials and reviews. Evie vouched for you, it's all we need. I have to run. Check your device. The ebook fairy sent you a few more gifts. Love ya.

Remember high school when you were delegated social cliques from your first day? The mean girls and jocks ruled the roost–popularity was hard-earned and it didn't come cheaply. Perform, conform, or you're a pariah. The Smut Mafia team requirements were no different.

I held on to the belief book chat was a good thing for six months. The patina gradually wore off, leaving a rusty edge, ready to slice deep, with every abusive message received.

The_Smut_Mafia_Chat.
Monday, January 25.

D.D.: @Gloria! What the fuck, it's Monday. Why didn't you hit the promo groups with Miranda's sale?

Gloria: I started work at 4 a.m. It's only 6 p.m. now. I still have a few hours.

D.D.: Look, if you can't get your shit together, I have people lined up to join this team. Y'all know we're elite.

Gloria: Give me time to feed the dogs. Get John's dinner on, and I'll start.

Ten minutes later my phone pings again.

D.D.: @Gloria! Seriously? How hard is it to get the post right?

Gloria: I shared in Luxe, Barbie's group. The hit list needs updating. Most groups are refusing to approve street team posts.

D.D.: I don't give a fuck where you posted, stupid bitch. It was *last* week's post! For fuck's sake, are you blonde or what?

Gloria:...

Gloria:...

Gloria has left the chat.

Evie: I dropped mine on all the blogs @DD.

D.D.: Thanks @Evie. Mwah.

Mel: Same @DD. I hit groups hard. A few double-ups. The newbies posted in mine. LOL. @Kat, you can ignore the top five in the list, they're SMC's.

Kat: @Mel ok, thanks for the heads up. Still new to this.

Mel: @Kat, all good, hon. You'll pick it up.

LM: Hey, @DD. Not cool. You know Gloria's struggling.

D.D.: I don't give a fuck. Rules apply, and you've committed to supporting my authors. Put up or shut up. She'll be back tomorrow after her tantrum. How many times now?

Debbie: Yeah, I'm with @LM. Not cool @DD.

D.D.: @LM @Debbie, y'all are replaceable too–don't forget.

Evie, Mel liked the comment.

D.D.: Anyhow, team catch-up, Market Mall, @ Beanz, on Friday @10. Let me know who's in. Y'all are welcome.

Evie: I've got the morning off. @Kat, I'll swing by and pick you up.

Kat: Ok? Sounds fun, I guess.

D.D.: I need to bitch slap a few groups before bed. Three books to finish tonight. Fuck my life and deadlines. Be back later.

Chapter Nine

Damon

Present

The holder of the key.

"Thanks for coming in, Kat. I wanted to run a few things by you, and thought the office was more time efficient."

Nadine knocks on the door, balancing a tray of coffee and danish. "As requested, Damon. Hi Kat, nice to see you again. The boss ordered in from the patisserie next to the bank and thought you'd enjoy a treat with coffee. Anything else Damon?"

"Thoughtful of you. That's all for now, thank you." Always the professional, she closes the door leaving us to resume our discussion. I pull up my edits, and the comments returned by Kat overnight, expanding on a few points.

She picks up her device and scrolls through my initial questions.

"OK, let's pick a trope, say dark romance. Implied, it's dangerous, forbidden, with criminal undertones. The temptation to exaggerate, out-write, and out-perform overrides common sense too often. Extreme levels of the macabre lie here. It's possibly the highest selling point in the indie romance genre. Add dark in your search strings and synopsis, you're guaranteed an instant following."

Kat hums in agreement, as she adds to her notes. "The term dark has been widely debated recently. The trend for inexperienced authors to classify their content as dark–they've abused the trope in doing so. Suspense or thriller is a better moniker in most cases."

"Agreed. If we're adding pet peeves, this one's mine. Younger readers believe they're reading *dark romance*, hype's told them so. Eventually, they come across the real deal, and slam the authors with one-star reviews because it terrifies them."

"These younger authors create imagined mafia families, weak-willed women, and masochistic heroes. They'll never come face to face with a one-percenter biker, or hold a knife and gut a rabbit—let alone wield it in blood play. Unfortunately, they're glorifying it in their novels without research." Her disgust at their lack of believable content ruffles her feathers every time and is evident in her sarcasm. "I know this one's a drama unfolding in groups everywhere. Google is infamous for providing subpar content, and it's as deep as most go. If you're going to string a bow, find the relevant historical data. The same applies to knives and metallurgy—a hunting knife is fantastic for rough work. Its blade isn't fine enough to filet a fish or manifest a slow bleeding arterial wound."

"The issue is, they refuse to research—damn prima donnas are above it. They skimp on details and just *write the stories* that come to them. Heaven forbid, they decide to include the idea of taboo. Siblings, parents, anything morally or biblically unacceptable, triggers a set of sales gimmicks involving content warnings."

Her grin widens, "Don't you mean triggers?"

"It's a phrase coined by indie authors. You'll never read a synopsis by a traditionally published writer referring to trigger warnings. Cancel culture has overstepped too often. Indie placate and bow to pressure, rather than make a stance, maintaining their voice. A trigger is personal. I detest clowns, so are they a trigger-worthy mention?"

Kat giggles, breaking into laughter. "Clowns? Oh my god, are you two?" I catch my breath mid-sentence, and her face falls at my reaction. Back peddling, her smile disappears. "Sorry. I apologize. That's extremely insensitive of me."

I attempt to hide my smirk, but images of clowns pack my head space like sardines in a Mini. "Apology accepted. No clown triggers in case you were wondering."

She relaxes back into the chair, and her cheeky grin reappears. "There's a website strictly designated to things people find triggering. The lists, independent authors share, they're content warnings—potential scenarios which may trigger a reader—rape, incest, abuse. The most confusing inclusion demanded in these warnings is the mention of cheating."

"Cheating? Are they teenagers? If you take a moral or biblical stance, reading romance would be deemed cheating on your partner. Any fictional adoration, or the book boyfriend habit, would tick that particular box."

"I'm always amused over the cheating reference appearing regularly in my social media group searches. It cracks me up every time I read non-cheating requests. I guess it's the age of readers more than the trope. Everyone cheats in some way. Insert the biblical idea, as you stated, reading romance equates to cheating–they're cheating and require non-cheating books." Her cheesy grin cracks glossed lips, chasing away the shadows again.

"Technically speaking, romance readers are entering into fictional relationships—inserting themselves into a book, replacing a hero or heroine. The notion books with characters who cheat need warnings is obsolete and comical. Hell, I was cheated on repeatedly and I love a good redemption story." Kat shifts positions, the sun hitting her hair like a halo. Glorious deep, cerulean blue eyes darken–luminous pools, gaze back, and intensify. She slides her finger over notes, drumming her left hand against her knee. A grimace creases her brows, and her lips narrow.

"So, cheating's amusing. Why the glum expression? You're heading off on a tangent I'm guessing. What else is bothering you? You mentioned in your email you wanted to dig deeper. In doing so, it may raise a red flag."

"Hell, I'm already up to my neck. The most concerning points are file control and content." Kat continues her rhythmic beat against the screen.

"Why? And by files, you're referring to the final manuscript? That face, by the way, is golden, so tell me how you honestly feel."

Her mood is mercurial today, flashing between concern and joy, she studies me intently. "Yep. The raw file is ready for upload for publication. You'd assume with piracy, authors would protect them with their lives, right?"

"Of course. Publishing anywhere before release voids contracts in many cases... It's a security issue. An open invitation to sell and pirate work for anyone in need of a quick dollar."

It's the reason we only send out arcs in a paperback version now. The quick resale of unprotected ebooks guaranteed they were online before release otherwise.

"But, what if the bloggers are the authors?" Her tone is

pensive, waiting for my response.

"Not possible, they're two separate entities. Bloggers are driven readers—we all know this. Blogs have been around forever."

The smug grin returns. "Legitimate readers, bloggers, and authors are all but extinct. This is the grievous offense we've permitted to occur right under our noses. It's a shell game, nothing more, nothing less." I watch her tap out a rapid cadence on her device, note-taking as she chats. "I'd estimate bloggers formally control the success of ninety percent of independent publications in the romance genre. They become authors, reviewers, promoters, cover designers, and photographers, all in one neat, tidy, exclusive package—out of necessity. It still amazes me no one else has worked it out."

Thrusting the screen in my face, she points at a graphic pyramid. "To blatantly flaunt the conspiracy, opens them up to the risk of detection."

Floored at the implications, the depth of her potential to cause chaos, I'm shocked it's so blatantly obvious. "How the hell did you uncover something so outrageous and unimaginable? Why didn't anyone question this sudden rise to fame of so many newcomers?"

"I guess it's why we're brainstorming my next outline, isn't it? But how much harm will outing someone do? And who'll be left standing in the rubble?"

"It's your story, you decide the narrative. How fine is this line between fact and fiction?"

"A hair's breadth."

"Are you sure this is the path you're willing to take? As much as I'm beyond flattered to be part of this in even the basest form, is it something you can live with?"

"Watching from stage left, as the drama unfolded? The

personal loss, mental health issues, and in my time—suicides. The question is, how can you live knowing you could have reached out and possibly prevented something?"

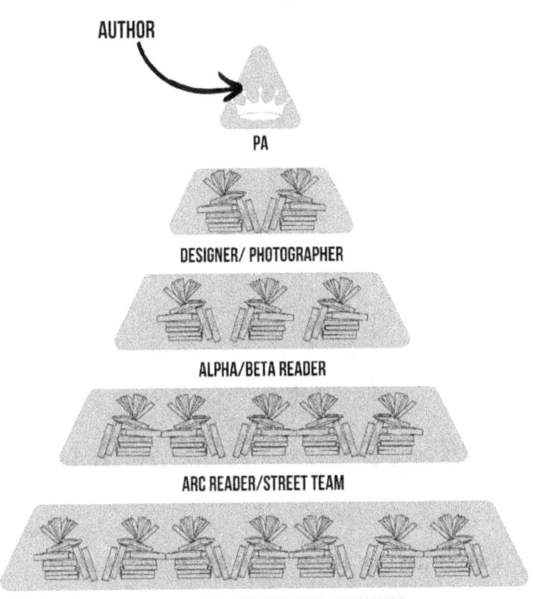

AXIS OF INDEPENDENT PUBLISHING TEAMS

Chapter Ten

Kat

Two years prior.

North Street Beanz, Friday 29th January.

My first coffee date with the team solidified my position with Dee, instantly.

"Orders, ladies?" Dee, phone ready, logged into the diner's app, was digging for loose change in her faded denim pockets.

"Let me. First time and all." I pull my credit card from my wallet, and the black card below slides out. My ears ring with the low whistle from Dee and her girls in unison.

"La-de-dah. Someone has a sugar daddy."

Raucous laughter, at my expense, surrounds me. "No, just a hard-working husband and my part-time job."

"Yeah right." Dee snarks. "Nothing says hard work like a black card." She runs her fingers over the raised numbers–I'm sorely tempted to snatch it back. "The party we could hold with this baby."

"Sorry, Dee. She's maxed out. Always is. Low interest and all."

There's a flash of something—anger or jealousy? It's not a pleasant look, on what's predominantly a beautiful facsimile of perfection.

"Whatever." Not calling me out directly, a shiver of apprehension warns me to tread lightly here. "Kat's treat, girls. What will it be?"

I wait patiently to include mine to the smorgasbord they've ordered; a regular skinny iced frappe and cinnamon toast. Handing over my card, Dee holds it against her phone, a quick nod, and the order disappears into cyberspace.

With a swift kick to the shin, I choke on my comment. Evie's mug rattles, frantically stirring extra sugar in her low-fat concoction. An imperceptible frown and quick save prevented my foot-in-mouth agenda.

This was the first of many *treats on Kat,* as our coffee and nights out became known.

Kat
Past

Home Sweet Home

Throwing my keys into the brass fish bowl on the entry table, I drop my coat on the rack beside the front door. *What a night.* I'm not sure how many more I'll manage, the girls are wearing me out.

Dale waits for me—the resigned expression I've witnessed too often lately, adorns his features. I catalog the once formidable man in front of me. He's let himself go. He used to sport a taught body, abs, and clean-shaven features. His hair's now sprinkled with gray, his dad-bod shows—he's not the man I married.

"You need a haircut, Dale. I'll book you in with the boys for Saturday." Alcohol, still buzzing through me, I ignore his grimace.

Eyes peruse my tightly bound frame. I've worked hard these last six months to recover some of my youth. I'm proud of the effort and commitment I made to myself–finally–with the support of Dee and her girls. I'm worthy, no one can tell me otherwise.

"Have you looked at yourself lately?" Frustration evident, his voice waivers. "Botox. Dental implants. Push-up bras. Midriff tops and leather pants. What sort of role model are you providing the boys? Women are not objects to lust over. They're not possessions to be displayed on a shelf, and taken out for erotic playtime."

A laugh bubbles up, overflowing my lips, and I'm unable to hold it in. "We're not in the fifties, Dale. I'm not chained to the sink–barefoot and pregnant—at your beck and call. To, how do you put it–*to pleasure you*–when you feel your cock size doesn't compare."

I watch the once familiar features morph into a stranger. The man I married after high school, was no longer my best friend and confidant. A speech bubble moment, straight out of a cartoon hits hard—I've outgrown him.

"It's fiction. Don't you understand this is an obsession? Your friends, as you call them, they're nothing more than influencers, using gullible women to further their agenda."

I expected rage coming in late. Not unfounded accusations.

"My friends? This is me. It's my body. My choice. If you can't appreciate the effort I've put in, you never saw me for who I was."

"You're broken. I see you—I understand more than you'll ever share with me. These girls, they're a bad influence, hon."

Dale's warm brown eyes shine with unshed tears. He's not been there for me these last few years. It's his hang-up, not mine.

"So, you're jealous of a few books, a coffee or two? Grow up, Dale."

Grabbing up my keys, he grips my wrist, bruising it–what's one more? Catching and chipping a nail in his haste to return my keys, he drags me closer; stale beer makes me gag. "I'm doing this for our kids–for the boys. I'm not raising men who'll objectify women. They're impressionable. Flaunting twenty-year-olds, made up like emo dolls under their noses–you've brought this drama into our lives, we don't need it."

"*Fuck this.*" I throw the keys back at the hall table. With a metallic ding, they hit the bowl and bounce off.

Dale's chest heaves with an indrawn breath. He waves his hand to the black case beside the front door. "You need to leave, hon." A tone I've not heard in years rumbles deep within his chest. I adored that deep timbre and dominance in his voice during sex, once upon a time.

"You've got to be *fucking* kidding me." Irate doesn't begin to address the feeling of betrayal fighting the voice of reason and aggression flooding my veins. "You can't kick me out of my own home, Dale. I'm not garbage being thrown to the curb."

"No, you're more than that. So much more. Until you recognize the danger you're in, the potential damage to our kids–you need to stay somewhere else."

His energy depleted, shoulders drop, and I almost miss the whispered prayer, "just until you come to your senses."

"If I pick up those keys, and walk out the door, we're over. You know it, I know it. Is this honestly what you want Dale?"

"You've given us no choice, Kat." The ever-present voice of

reason, Dale drops his eyes to mine. "While you're associating with book teams, playing personal assistant for below minimum wage, you're not with us. The porn playing over the speakers when the boys walked in? Jaimie's dad was beside himself over it. He wanted to know what we're teaching our kids."

"Porn? Really? It's literature, maybe a little smut, but they're best-selling books. Have you written a bestseller with over one million page reads lately?"

I wait patiently, this I know. I'm capable of defending my job, my friends, and their art. No one gets to label it porn.

"They're selling sex for profit. Simple. You're pushing it like a pimp. Pimping is the term, isn't it? I'm correct, aren't I?"

"You're right this time," I huff. The reference to pimping reminds me of Adra's book, ready to promo. Crap, I almost forgot after the last margarita. Dee asked me to check my scheduling, and see if I had room for an additional book this week. "We're not pimps, literally. You make it sound tawdry. The term is *influencer*."

"You hit the nail on the head. You're influencing a generation trapped in their own homes by a virus. Captive audience, if you will—pushing pornography to minors, and anyone in earshot."

I watch Dale push the luggage toward me. The glossy black case mirrors my reflection. Tucking a wayward lock of hair back in place, I fish lip a pout, sucking my cheeks in.

"See! You're always on. There's no camera. No selfie op. You're obsessed with your reflection in a suitcase for Christ's sake."

"Blaspheme, much? What would your momma say, Dale?"

With a gentle shove, the luggage rolls into my knee. If I pick it up...

"I've booked rooms at The Maryitaville, long-term. The housekeeping and meals are paid for upfront. You need to reassess your place in our lives. I've canceled your black card. I've left the Cyber, still active. The credit limit remains at ten, I paid it off for you, and won't again."

Reality slaps me in the face sitting outside The Maryitaville.

An attractive young bellhop waits beside the entrance, the valet opens my door, hand extended for my keys. Grabbing a ten from my wallet, I hand it over as he takes my car.

I'm on my own for the first time since I was eighteen. No Dale. No kids. No imaginary white picket fence surrounding the brownstone, defending me from the outside world. My fairytale bubble exploded, with one final drink.

Flicking the coffee pot on, the last hours are a blur. I spin slowly, taking in my surroundings. The rooms are conventional, with pristine white rugs, and a light-colored sofa. The bland cream laminate kitchen, with its dull stainless stove and sink, isn't the standard I'm accustomed to.

My single luggage item sits in the middle of a black, oriental duvet. Popping the latch, the basics are meticulously packed, rolled army style. Dale managed to include everything I'd have considered for a two-week vacation.

Nestled in the bottom, an antique framed family portrait glares accusingly. The boys were all at school, Bobby missing a front tooth, displaying a gapped grin. Rabbit ears are held behind him by Ben. Bobby smiles sweetly into the camera, oblivious to his brother's antics.

I've always been there for them. Threw away my youth and education, to raise the boys. I gave up my editing job with a local newspaper, six months into my first pregnancy, and Dale's first prominent posting—all while he played tin soldier and officer, with his buddies. At least his parents' political clout granted us stability and a home. I wasn't raised to be an army wife, moving base to base. Liaison, for the last few years, meant I was on parental duty twenty-four-seven.

This is my time to shine. Dale doesn't understand. He's toured the world numerous times, and I stayed home, holding the fort.

I wish him well, reigning in three teenage terrors.

Chapter Eleven

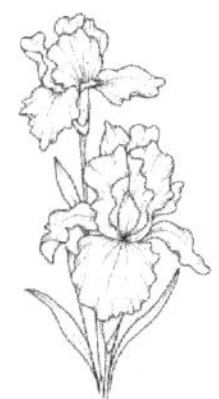

Kat

Two years prior.

The_Smut_Mafia_Chat. Monday, February 8.

DD.: Happy Monday everyone. Let's get the week off to a positive start and clear out the negatives. Pet peeve, ladies?
Kat: Song and brand references are used repeatedly.

Smiley faces appear from all bar Dee.

DD.: But it's important to set the scene. You need to know what they're wearing, eating, and drinking.
Kat: Understood, but name-dropping is so high school. Think mean girls. Who cares if every female lead snorts powder, it's so seventies. In ten years are you going to remember the Aussie beer, Corona? There's a song too. It dates the book.
D.D.: It's how we do it. My team, my rules.
Evie: Can you explain further, @DD?

... dots appear. Is she serious? The belief readers only comprehend content associated with brand names is ludicrous. Evie was on my side going into this, or so I believed.

D.D.: My authors. My teams. These are the books being written. You'll read, and keep your ideas to yourself.

Kat: Ok! I'm wrong in my assumption then this was just a book club. Reading because we love to? Now, as a collective, we're assisting with writing the novel too. So, do we receive credit for content?

D.D.: ROFL. The combined amount all of you contribute is negligible.

Kat: But…

D.D.: No buts. It's not a democracy. As a beta reader, you have the list. Strip down any issues, and export your electronic device notes to Libby's email address. Don't forget to copy me on it too."

Kat: Why Dee? It's not like you're a PA or anything. You keep telling us you do this all for free.

Likes pop up from everyone, bar Evie. We discussed this at length last night. I thought she had my back–I just have to wear it now.

Kat: @Evie?

D.D.: Rules are simple. You're here to read, note, and break down the plot.

Gloria: Can you highlight blocks of words, not just one or two? I can't find them to edit.

Kat: It's why I export notes. You have the location in the file too.

Gloria: It takes me hours to go over suggestions once I find them. For your information @Kat, most aren't errors.

Kat: Typos, repetition, and grammar aren't errors? Since when?

Gloria: Normal people skim over them. You're not reading effectively, you're wanting the book to fail.

Kat: Seriously? So, your little piece of paper…I don't want your job if it's what you're scared of.

Gloria: Distinction. I came first in my class.

Kat: Distinction then. That degree makes you an expert, right off the bat?

Gloria: Remember, I'm published. You're not. Your limited knowledge and reading experience don't amount to much here.

The chat screen fills up with inappropriate memes and gifs. The die-hard sheep follow their leader.

Kat: Yeah, fine. Back in my place. Cheers xx.

D.D.: @Kat Don't forget, highlights and screenshots. Don't bother sending without.

Last word. Always the last word.

Kat
Present.

Kat's notebook: Notes on consistency and realism.

The unwritten rule in book club is never to read the same trope you're writing. It also applies to movies and television shows. The human mind unintentionally regurgitates information onto the written page, equating to familiar plots. Monkey see monkey do attitude, intentional or not, mimicry exists.

Made for TV is rarely an accurate portrayal of medicine, crime organizations, or police action. They can't disclose in-depth protocols. Research assistants are utilized—accessing the fields portrayed, ensuring continuity, and a realistic approach to contemporary subjects we're familiar with. As my grandmother said, research, my dear, is key. Never assume readers are ignorant. Authors, after all, were readers themselves.

There's no pedestal placing a published author above another human being, contrary to the belief of so many. We all bleed alike at the end of the day.

Never take a reader for granted. Who they appear to be on screen, and their real-life experience—you may receive a rude shock.

Chapter Twelve

Damon

Present.

Taste, touch, smell. Rape and pillage of content.

Writing is a solitary pursuit. If anyone tells you otherwise—they're not performing to their full potential.

Craft takes time to establish and evolve. Sentence structure, grammar, pace, depth—endless components required to execute a manuscript, don't occur overnight. Many hold tertiary education degrees, so in theory, anyone can write. Sadly, more often than not, it's a case of should they?

I'm in awe daily at the extent some will go to achieve celebrity status. The drive and persistence required to put one's self in the firing line to submit a manuscript, setting themselves up for rejection.

Scanning my emails, there's a message from our contracts department outlining Kat's commitment, and our formal agreement to work together for three books. Dropping a quick email, with revisions, I suggest a coffee meet-up tomorrow to touch base and check on progress.

I look forward to playing mentor and leading her through the complexities of publishing with us. Even more, I'm interested in peeling the layers from the enigma presented to me on a platter.

This woman intrigues me like no other.

"Kat, You look fantastic." I lean in and kiss her cheek, taking the seat across from her.

A blush, reminiscent of a teenager, hit her high cheekbones, and her face lit up at my approach. Hair pulled back, in a ponytail, wearing a soft flowing paisley dress, she'd pass for ten years younger.

"You too, Damon. Great choice of venue. I've not been out in daylight this week." Dropping her voice, she leans in, sliding a nail along my palm. "Good thing I don't combust in sunlight."

I chuckle at our ongoing debate about glittering immortals and the far-fetched vampire series she adores. I'm yet to meet another who's utterly addicted to unfeasible, teenage sit-com movies.

"I enjoyed the edits, thanks. Resolved points regarding flow in my copy, annotated in the comments for you."

A caramel latte and maple bacon donut arrive. Her herbal tea and cinnamon toast are a stark contrast to my indulgent treat. "Thanks, Kat, I needed a sugar fix today."

"This early, my guess is you've missed breakfast trying to accommodate me. Sorry to put you out."

I grasp her fingers, manically drumming a beat only she can hear. Her pulse feels erratic, her skin cool to the touch. "Are you ok,

Kat? You'll let me know if we push too hard?"

With an imperceptible nod, she pulls her fingers away, rubbing her hand—removing my touch unconsciously. "As recommended, I've removed myself from the temptation to reconnect with my team. I've deleted every point of influence or mutual friend online."

Playing on her mind, this explains her silence over the last few days. Her eyes meet mine, her smile not quite reaching them, she continues. "Back to those bullet points. I've backed up our shared folder. I agree with your side notes that they lack due diligence, failing the reader's need for accurate research. You can't include suspense or thriller without realism. I suspect it's another loophole they've attempted, to include their high *smut perspective* as you've labeled it, while avoiding the thirty percent cut-off dumping it in erotica. I don't want to be labeled in that basket, thank you."

"The adage is a bullet won't fire around a corner. A scene will be torn apart for years to come over the presumption readers won't notice the finer details. They forget, if you load it, the plot expects it to be fired. It's simply how things work. If you pull a knife to cut a zip tie, leaving it beside the character, it's implied you'll use it for something further on."

Nodding in agreement, she recognizes my input is critical, but necessary. "The path is laid out–there's a formula applied, be it romance, suspense, or fantasy. There are rules. It's rare for an author to break the mold. You don't reinvent the wheel–rules are the threads holding literature together. The written word is literature, regardless of genre or trope. Without rules—they're random words entwined on a page."

"In theory, we're taught this in creative writing courses, as far back as high school. Cause and effect, I understand the basics and principle."

"Of course you do." A smug grin appears. She pulls her bottom lip in, releasing an audible pop, and a muffled giggle. "You understand as you're educated–it's drummed into your psyche. You can't expect a reader to connect and comprehend a storyline if the author has zero formal training or natural storytelling ability. Even then, there's a vast difference between a skilled writer and one who's studied and merely executes a technically average plot."

"Just because you can write..."

Kat completes my sentence. "Doesn't mean you should."

"The question remains, are they capable of pulling it off? Most certainly not."

"This remained one of my biggest issues with the team. Feed them free books, they weren't concerned about quality or source– just their names in the acknowledgments."

Chapter Thirteen

Kat

Past

One year prior.

You know the little voice in the back of your mind? The one telling you right from wrong? Mine lies— it lay broken on the rocks below, many years ago. Instead of preventing me from stepping into the road–I crossed the lines, and walked right in front of the crazy train.

The most heartbreaking thing in all of this? I believed Evie was a friend and confidant.

The_Smut_Mafia_Chat.

Thursday 11th June

D.D.: New author, ladies. There's a free back catalog to read. Follow her profile on all platforms.
Kat: Question?
D.D.: Of course you do, @Kat. What?

Mina: ROFL burn baby. She knew it was coming.

Kat: Another? I'm swamped right now. Can I pass and come back to it?

D.D.: You want off the team @Kat? Is it too hard to read a few books for your friends?

Kat: No. I'm over-committed this month. Between edits, two reads, and arcs…

D.D.: Three 25k novellas. It's an evening's read. Fuck. I managed six books today, how many did you contribute?

Kat: What the fuck? Six? How is that possible? No one reads six books in a day.

D.D.: Slow day. What can I say? You pick up your reader, open the first page, and read. Doesn't take a degree to work it out.

Kat: But six? You're not reviewing them?

D.D.: Fuck yeah, I am. Easy. Rotate a few old reviews in, and insert the character names. They're all five stars anyway.

Kat: Won't someone notice? You can't rely only on vague reviews, can you?

The screen fills with smileys. I guess I am naïve.

D.D.: Seriously? We read twenty-plus books a week and you thought reviews would be original? Where did you come from, babe?

Kat: So read the book, fill in character names, and.

D.D.: Read the book? Are you for real? You skim. Flick through the first few chapters, jump to the middle, and read the last two or three.

Kat: But your device knows the page reads, the percentage.

D.D.: I don't give a fuck what their app says–my account's banned. I'm only interested in review sites, the top three. No one reads the distributor website reviews.

Kat: How did I not know this? So, let me get it straight, you supply bogus reviews?

Mina: Umm @Kat, bogus isn't accurate–mine are legit.

D.D.: Back in your box @Mina. No one asked you. @Kat it's how we do it. It's always been this way. Twenty to fifty fluffy words, how much you loved it, nonspecific, and no spoilers.

Kat: But I'm not going to one-click a book based on your bland review. 'Twists and turns,' what exactly are they supposed to be?

D.D.: Yeah, you are. Like the rest of the sheep, desperate for a handout. You'll click. You'll read and review in the same format as the rest of us. No one wants your opinion. You don't need to analyze a book.

Kat: I understand we have to review and summarize efficiently. It's a product, so consumers want honest, verified purchase reviews. Don't they?

D.D.: @Evie, I thought you said she was smart? My cat has more brain cells.

Evie: @Kat, just go with it. @D.D. She understands indie as a business. She's made more authors than Crush PR.

D.D.: MWAH @Evie. Love your face xxx

Kat: Fine, send the links through. I'll find time this weekend.

D.D.: Nah, tonight. You're behind on Razz's books. These take priority. Ok?

Kat: I guess, I'll find the time.

D.D.: Too easy. Now, back to our next discovery. This took a lot of time to dig out, but I think we're on to a winner. Check out the blurb, ladies.

What if everything you've—
Bought. Devoured. Flaunted.
In the last three years was,
Phony. Repurposed. Poisoned.
Still ready to smash that promo button?
Eyeball the guts?
Scour for ripped plots and lines?
We sure as hell did.
Strap in—there's a wild ride ahead.
Armour up those big-girl undies; mess incoming.
Indie publishing, meet your mirror.
#smutmafiagate beckons.

Chapter Fourteen

Kat

Present.

Mind, heart, and soul.

I press the buzzer before I chicken out. Two pizzas balanced on my hip complete with sides, I pray Damon's forgiven me for my abrupt exit this morning. Flashbacks drive my muse, but they take every spare ounce of energy from me.

As I turn to leave, the door flies open, Damon's exasperation quickly turning to pleasure. I slide my eyes down his damp skin, stopping at the happy trail, delving into the towel wrapped around his hollowed hips. The connection sparks again and is pleasantly unexpected. I'd long since thought my body was immune to the basics of attraction, human chemistry, and insta love as they say.

The L word? Where the hell did that come from?

"My favorite author comes bearing gifts," he drawls, tipping an imaginary cap. I burst out laughing at his amiable expression and easygoing nature.

"Supper for my lord and master, small penance for the trouble I caused today." Happy to follow his lead, I duck below the arm bracing the door frame, as he waves me through.

"After you m'lady. Give me a moment to change."

I watch Damon's tight glutes beneath the towel, he spins checking my attention is still his. I blush like a teenager when the wet towel is thrown out through the bedroom door. Knowing he's naked just a few feet away sets off alarm bells and sends my pulse into overdrive.

Damon

Kat downed the last of her chardonnay, unfurling her body from the comfortable depths of the sofa. "Fancy another, Damon? It's Friday after all." My brief acknowledgment sends her racing into the kitchen to grab a fresh bottle. Popping the cork, my glass ready, with a flourish, she plays waitress.

"You raised worrisome tropes this morning, how could they present someone's lifestyle without sensitivity readers? Even an ingénue in indie would understand the importance of being politically correct."

"They didn't. Zero checks are in place to prevent blowouts with glaringly unfamiliar topics. Snide terms were used out of context; I may skirt the edges, I'm not ignorant of the lingo." Cracking her neck, I watch the flex of her shoulders, attempting to relieve the tension built up from days of self-editing.

A thought niggles at the back of my mind, "I'll be right back." Digging through my hallway cupboard, I unearth a still-wrapped gift. Quickly divesting it of its packaging, I plug the oil warmer in beside the sofa. Dropping cushions between my feet, I pat the floor encouraging Kat to move closer. Honey, cinnamon, and sweet citrus tease my senses, comforting and familiar at once.

A dirty grin and she's seated between my knees, legs pulled up to her chest, propped up on the cushions. "Please tell me we're not moving into the realms of cheesy book porn?"

I don't have the heart to remind her she's the novelist, and I'm the editor who promotes said cheesy book porn for her.

"No book porn. Nothing cheesy. Think of this as research. I'll just jump-start your muse tonight."

A breathy giggle leaves her lips, and the minute vibration from a moment of calm reverberates through me.

Laying the towel across my legs, I push the straps down her bare arms. Tipping warmed oil into my cupped palm, I drizzle it between Kat's shoulders. Sliding one hand lower, I trail down the small of her back. The sweet almond oil releases its heady, relaxing mixture on contact with her warm skin.

Gently, I knead her shoulders, working into taught muscle, knotted from days spent over a keyboard.

"God, Damon. Where did you learn your technique?" My name, on her breathy groan, sends impulses shooting to areas I'm not taking advantage of.

"Rehab," bursts from me, before I can stop my misfiring brain.

Kat stills below my ministrations. I almost miss her muffled, "I'm sorry." Reaching out, I grasp her proffered fingers gently. "If you want to talk about it, or not..." The comfort evoked by her simple touch keeps me in the present.

"Another time, Kat." Releasing, I add more oil to her toned skin, her comfort, my sole aim tonight. "We have plenty of time."

I work my way gradually down her spine. Rolling knuckles along muscles, working deep into her skin, in a combination of tried and trusted methods. I lose myself in the companionable silence, broken occasionally by Kat's groan, as I pass over particularly tense areas.

Dropping a blanket over her warm muscles, I lean back into the sofa. She collapses next to me propping her bare feet on my lap.

Playfully, I run a forefinger along her sole, eliciting a jump and giggle. "You're still with me then, gorgeous?"

"Only just. I needed this, Damon. I'd happily melt into the bed and die a happy woman right now."

"No dying here tonight, hon." Grasping her down pointed toes, I work the oil into her feet, slowly.

"Heaven, I'm in heaven," she sing-songs, ending on a hum. "Foot fetish, anyone?"

"Why am I not surprised you enjoy your feet being played with? Must be the plethora of shoes you attempt to hide."

"Give a girl one addiction. It's not like I have..." I slide my fingers between her exquisitely kept toes, as her sigh completes her thought process, "others."

"My girl likes that?" Pleased with my unplanned move, relaxed and at ease, I'm surprised how readily she accepted tonight's change of pace.

"Your girl loves this. I'm going to need to discover what other secrets you're hiding in your repertoire I suspect."

Ever so slowly, I work my way up her calves, discovering how ticklish she is behind her knees. Hitting the edge of her dress, Kat shifts, arching her back, stretching languorously.

"Don't stop, Damon. I'm not running this time."

The green light goes straight to my cock–he's not received the message—this is my gift tonight, not his.

Loose ends and frayed edges aren't my thing—continuity and reliable content, I crave– I'm not letting her leave unfulfilled.

Kat

Wrapped in the warmth of the wine, the accomplishment of handing in my manuscript; skilled hands run over my fevered skin—my week just hit five stars. I grasp the hand tentatively gliding below my skirt, stilling Damon's move forward.

"I'm going to take that as a no then," the disappointment in his voice wakes me from my haze.

"Hmm no, Damon. I'm not putting the brakes on." I wave at the expensive leather sofa beneath us. "Perhaps we take this to…"

Without a moment's hesitation, I'm swept up into muscular arms, and he paces towards his bedroom. Elbowing the door open, I groan at the vision of the four-poster walnut bed and brocade satin bedspread. Soft lighting throws shadows, as I'm laid on the expansive surface.

"Give me a moment." Damon spins on his heels. Returning, his grin stretched wide, the oil warmer finds its way to the bedside table. A wrapped, hotel-style robe accompanies an assortment of treats and another bottle of chardonnay.

Eager for this to continue, I slide the zip of my skater dress down further, swapping it for the soft terry robe; it smells like vanilla and roses, teasing my heightened senses.

Damon gently brushes my fingers from the exploration of gray sweatpants, tented by his erection—they're a turn-on—who knew?

"My treat tonight. We're celebrating you." His gravelly voice hints at his restraint, I clench my thighs in anticipation. "Last chance."

Moving up the bed, giving Damon access, I hand over the control he seeks. Slick fingers find their way to my panties, removing them, hooded eyes, waiting for my response.

"Please," my breathy moan, begs him to finish what he's started.

Gliding further up my thigh, I whimper. Anticipation, heady, the thought of his mouth overwhelms my senses—he delves in, lips crushing mine.

Warmth floods my body, eager for contact, I push my hips to him, the friction elicits a groan from his gorgeous throat. I run my fingers down his back, grasping his ass with my other hand, thrusting up into him.

"Please, Damon."

"I'm loving this side of you my little cat. All eager for me." He groans against my throat, nipping the tender flesh, fingers gliding downward, followed by greedy lips.

Glorious friction hits my clit, finally. A tentative exploration begins. Eagerly I rub myself against him. Pushing my hand into his waistband, needing to return the favor, Damon grabs my wrist. "Not tonight, Kat. This one's for you—only you."

Nodding, I acquiesce. Brain misfiring, engulfed by long-forgotten pleasure, I settle in for the ride.

Damon's tongue replaces digits, in a desperate rhythm, running from clit to entrance. Warm, tingling sensations threaten to send me into the abyss, only to be withdrawn just as I threaten to fall over the cliff. Edging me closer each time, I'm desperate to reach the peak.

Grabbing Damon's hair, I redirect his attention to my target, my only thought—the finish line.

Fingers brush sensitive nerve endings, entering, curling upward, as he suctions my clit—waves of pleasure crash over me. His ministrations continue, slowing, his hips dry hump the mattress.

A culmination of alcohol, food, and satisfaction—engulfed by the pillowy softness of his bed—I melt into the luxurious thread count.

A warm, wet cloth replaces his mouth, and the residue of our passion is washed away. Damon's weight disturbs my post-coital high, pulling me to him, covering us. I'm lulled into sleep, his fingers gently tracing my tattoos, with his hard-on resting in the crease of my cheeks.

A cacophony of noise wakes me, reaching for my alarm, I come up empty. Light filters through the curtains. I forgot to pull my blinds down again last night, but the slats covering the window aren't unfamiliar.

The smell of coffee tempts me. As the memory of last night's events unfolds, I scramble for my discarded clothing, which is mysteriously absent. Finding a well-worn college tee on the end of the bed, I shrug into it and search out the appetizing aroma.

Chapter Fifteen

Damon

Present

Disheveled, Kat wanders out in my favorite tee. I love the feeling of contentment waking up with her beside me. It's the best night's sleep I've had in years. "Good morning, beautiful. Hope you slept well."

Kat's hand wraps around my shoulder, pulling me toward her. Reaching up, she drops a quick kiss on my lips, sliding her tongue along the seam. "Hmm, morning to you too D. Coffee tastes amazing." Her voice sends tingles down my spine. Grabbing a cup, she helps herself, sliding onto the seat at the breakfast bar.

Stacking pancakes between us, we settle into an amicable silence. Her appreciation of the simple meal comes complete with sounds of contentment, devouring syrup-covered carbs.

Cleaning up, she breaks the companionable silence, delving straight back into the ever-spinning maelstrom of her mind, and work.

"What if it's not real? What if Romancelandia is entirely contrived? Threats and rumors are traded between players, to drive up book sales when one falters. What if it's all a game, and readers fall for it?"

"You think it's contrived? A front for what exactly?"

"The sisterhood is tight, they'll tell you this—authors support authors—have each other's backs. More like, they hold your shoulders and look you in the eye, while friends line up to sink the knife in deep. Heaven forbid you sin and step out of line. They hijack your work, mass report, one-star review, or begin hate campaigns and rumors online."

I ponder her point, it's valid. To an outsider, the drama appears far-fetched. "Go on, this train of thought makes sense."

"Yeah, cause nothing else does. So, a crumb is dropped in a reader chat, something like 'Did you hear about—the characters are the same—the plot—whilst the perpetrators hide in plain sight as best sellers.' We'll try this example."

"Sure. Everyone's picked up on gossip, readers and authors alike." I can see the cogs working over time, heading down a path I'd contemplated, yet never voiced. "What's bothering you? Please tell me you've avoided reactivating your social media and not reconnected with them?"

A guilty grin appears. "No. Not really. I checked in on my family briefly and made the mistake of checking groups." Rubbing her nape, Kat licks her lips, throwing herself back into the fray. "The narcissistic public service announcements against other authors were mind-blowing."

"PSA's? Surely no one would forget they're a part of a larger community who don't forget." Restraint on public posts and censoring professional image would be of paramount concern.

"You'd hope so, but switching from best friend to hate-filled opponent, complete with orchestrated attacks overnight is common. Obliterating any semblance of professionalism, their ugly inner self is visible for all.”

“How is the behavior accepted by their peers, let alone readers? I can’t imagine how devastating it must be for their fan base to witness. The author-reader connection is one to be valued, not abused.”

“Factions split. The instigators rise and become activists. Pre-orders fold, and time’s wasted antagonizing rather than writing. Production falls behind. It’s assumed those they’ve run into the ground were the ones capable of navigating the mess on their behalf.”

“And? Who do they blame? At some stage, they’ll have to take responsibility for their immature actions.”

“Hell no. They pull the mental health card. In true narcissistic fashion—play the victim and aren’t mature enough, to accept actions have consequences. Insert new pen names, new blogger names, or resurrection of previous accounts. They put a two-year-old’s temper tantrum to shame.”

“Where are their fan bases in all of this? You’d hope someone intervenes and redirects the behavior, or has the sense to calm the situation.”

“Picking sides? Authors, friend fans who share their work, though it’s not osmotic, readers are another tool to be used. There’s no delineation between professional and business for the uninitiated. Any attempt to rein them in comes with argument.” Ardent in her stance, Kat’s voice doesn’t waiver. “Fans are running far from the noise. Online bullying is rampant in the book world. It becomes blatantly obvious who the driving force is behind the scenes when things don’t go their way. The meek, mild, hard done by victims personify unprofessionalism.”

“You’ve sat on the sidelines bearing witness, or is it all speculative?”

"As witness—caught in the crossfire, once too often. They don't back down and admit fault. Self-destructive and immature —too often it's the hand who fed them. The only way they'll learn is when their income suffers."

"You realize the question we couldn't uncover might be contained in this drama. The reason why the elite are blossoming. Those who've climbed the pyramid with little effort, seemingly out of thin air, arose and were crowned queens. The significant question—the one keeping me up at night—how was the queen of the day chosen? Were they simply easy to manipulate? Seduced by promises of devout fandom and money? Were they talented enough to get their foot in the door first—an honest to god unicorn—sparkling regally, in a sea of post-apocalyptic desperation? Or, were they willing to sell every moral—their soul —for a spotlight, no matter how brief?"

"How were these mere mortals chosen for greatness, elevated as higher beings? It wasn't talent-based, free reading platforms provide superior wordsmiths and craftsmanship. It all came down to how far they'd bend over, percentages, and the right team manipulating algorithms."

"I don't know why it's tolerated. I'm assuming because it's all built on one indiscretion after another?"

"Who honestly knows? Romancelandia, as a machine, is a well-honed tool. The minions took a bite and became rabid dogs. Nothing alleviated their hunger until they turned upon each other, destroying all implied threats. Think of a queen bee, and a hive full of aggressive drones. One intent and purpose– her survival–at their cost. Drones are just cannon fodder for the greater good–or the queen's ego."

"Back to my earlier point. How the hell was she chosen? Is it a rotation, do they share time in the public eye and charts equally, or do the submissive authors all bow down to one?"

"I think control is fading. Watching recent releases, some appear to have gone off script."

"You don't say." His chuckle warms me, defrosting some of the ice on the edges of my soul. "A number one best seller in store, it's a tad off script. I watched feeds and rants by bloggers. It's not her time. They're fraying at the edges, Kat."

"Interesting take. Can I use it?"

"With pleasure. All yours."

"One puppet master. Simple. Whoever created the monster comes back to a single idea. The fucking monster is knocking at my door. Do I let it in–offer it a sanctuary–or do I slay it?"

"My concern remains if we decide to remove it, who takes its place?"

"Better the devil you know, right?"

Chapter Sixteen

Kat

Present

J.D. Publishing, release week.

Peace, love, and book thieves.

Seated in Damon's office, coffee at the ready, a pot waiting; we've settled in for a day's work, comparing my new outline and updates on progress. My thought process is random at this stage, ideas and memories hit hard, and they're not ones I'm happy airing. "Did you notice an influx of new multi-author reader groups during lockdown?"

"No. It's not a traditional ideal. There's no control of the narrative. Author pages on social media, for sure, groups? Pass."

"They're start-ups."

Damon's pensive look concerns me. I'm not sure if I've gone too far–if he considers it a pure conspiracy. "Sounds ominous."

"A PA team of friends gets together, starts a new book group and combines resources. Let's call it XYZ."

"The basis or need for yet another of the thousands of indie groups is?"

"Control. PAs bring with them a multitude of sins. Few are qualified. Hint, they add PA to their first name and rarely use a surname–or it's an alias. They'll tell you they work as a hobby, or for free. Never believe the propaganda, they're being paid. Indie authors believe they won't survive without a PA." I was hit with this on arrival in the community and fought hard at each turn.

"Giveaways come with signed books. The latest fraud swaps ebooks in lieu of physical copies for international winners. No winner's names are disclosed due to 'privacy laws,' or they are non-active group members. You can pick the winners the moment the post appears. Often the same person wins multiple times in a takeover."

"I see where you're going with this now." No, he doesn't.

"It's either an alias or one of the PAs. So, incentives for their work they're paid in signed books."

"Don't readers cotton on to this?"

"Those who do are shut down, warned, or moderated. Some are banned from groups without warning if they raise questions." Many readers complained on platforms they'd been removed from groups, without the author being aware, the past few years.

"This PA business. Do they wake up one morning and decide they're what? Trained in marketing, business management, editing, and every aspect of the author trade? Where do they find these clowns?"

"Readers evolve into arc team members, then street teams, usually. Same readers see dollar signs and believe they can do better than those running the show–a promise they're incapable of delivering."

"What are we talking about price-wise? Per month, per event? Hourly rate?"

"All very hush, hush, open to negotiation. Unlike a legitimate agency, rates don't appear to be readily available. There's always been gossip, undercut the big five, they'll go after you hard."

Damon's phone vibrates across his desk. He takes the call, quickly and efficiently, approving an appointment change to free up his day with me.

Referring to his notes, one of many we've avoided arises. "We've said it before, words are infinite, are they not? So, answer me this, why must authors rehash the same plot outlines?" Damon's question, as always, is hard-hitting.

My next tangent might be harder to accept. "There's no copyright on plots or ideas. It's impossible to prove a concept has been stolen unless they're stupid enough to quote it verbatim. The plot manufacturers get away with their business selling plots because of a loophole. " I'm still amazed such a devious system exists in groups on free platforms, openly selling plots, concepts, and outlines. "It's a morally ambiguous stance, suggesting you can't protect plots, honestly. Writers write—they're creators. Where is the joy of replicating, or reinventing someone else's work? It's the fairytale retelling genre, all over again. Been there, done that, added a touch of gore, or kink, swap a trope, many live on the proceeds of public domain works. There's no joy in reading this scenario with a guaranteed ending." I detest the mass-produced, repetitive rubbish.

"I'd liken it to watching reruns. Imagine only having access to five episodes of a television show, day in and day out." With a harsh chuff of amusement, Damon gets my point.

"Exactly! Thank goodness someone else understands my insane soapbox. If words are infinite, why pray tell, don't authors utilize their god-given brains? You'd appreciate money spent on original content over…"

"Plagiarized work," Damon completes my sentence. We're in sync, and the easy nature of our relationship further validates my thoughts, easing my mind. I'm not being irrational over a slight on the craft, others openly accept.

"Therein lies the crux of the matter, and the source of outrage if readers cotton on to the scheme." He's right, of course.

"Why haven't they? It's glaringly obvious it's occurred for many years. Why aren't they outed for their behavior?"

I've dreaded this particular question, it's now or never. "Because, those involved constantly skirmish, running interference, generating drama and distraction. The public thrives on confusion and imagined slights, as fans. Haven't you noticed, as soon as one unbelievable offense occurs, it dies down, immediately replaced by another?"

"Putting it like that, yes. It appears to be an ongoing issue. I still don't understand why. How is it remotely productive to be at each other's throats, constantly?"

"Because they benefit financially on all levels. The root of all evil remains the dollar. What does it cost to buy a promotion, get in, and get out, before anyone's the wiser? Before the general population picked up an issue, the pen name's retired, and their LLC's gone. Ghosted."

"So, genius, what's the next trope and target?"

"Current remains sex trafficking with the criminal underworld playing savior, and a hint of suspense." Nothing new there, it's run for three years.

"What's your prediction for next year then?"

"Too easy—BDSM. Haven't you heard? Kink's stepped out of

the closet at last."

⁂

Kat
Past

The_Smut_Mafia_Chat. Monday, February 8.

Coffee and sweet nothings.

D.D.: Book tour, ladies. Ebook fairy delivery is on its way. Make sure to post promo in groups and everywhere you have access. Don't forget to jump onto the tour pages, comment, like, save, and share each other's posts.

Kat: Quick run down, please. Explain how this works, please. I'm sorry, I can't read another dull human trafficking knockoff with Stockholm syndrome falling in love with her rapist who's not a bad guy.

D.D.: It's not. Previously classified as erotica, it's now under suspense/thriller. Simple. The book sits under fifty reviews, so we're here to boost them. However, a new plan of attack for those who can still review on the big A. Drop four-star reviews, but in the review, state it's five.

Kat: Why? I'm not interested in manipulating data. It's not worth risking my account. I've lost it before over arcs.

D.D.: For fuck's sake, @Kat do it.

Kat: I'm asking why I can't put five stars if it's worth our time. Time is money, as you're always pointing out.

D.D.: The new algorithms! They break up reviews between verified and unverified. Currently, it doesn't distinguish between an arc and a discounted account trial. You know, the first month free, or three months at half price.

Kat: I remember. They don't appear as verified during the freebie. So, fine. Doesn't explain why a four-star rating benefits.

D.D.: It's pushed through immediately and not held hostage on your account. Fives take days, a four-star boosts instantly and gives a more realistic rating percentage. It comes up as a suggestion and feels more 'real'.

Kat: So it appears organic rather than a fake ranking? Readers won't click a plethora of five stars, they're looking for varied, right? Won't they query an older book with a rush of new reviews?

D.D.: Nope.

I swear she's in her element convinced I'm just a dumb reader–a captive audience to her charms. Lull her into believing we're complying, the shark appears every time.

D.D.: Remember, we tell them what to read. Cut and paste a few legitimate fan comments into your review this time.

Kat: So, I'm not sticking to my standard review shuffle?—just grabbing a few quick bites from others.

D.D.: Exactly.

Kat: Won't people realize? And, crap, posts. I keep forgetting popular groups won't accept your stock standard promo post, sorry.

L.B: Yeah, change your time. Ideas? They need to come across as fan girling, I've noticed a move in several chats.

Evie: It's the same when a dozen people recommend an older book or the first in a series in a group.

L.B: Yeah, those posts feel off. I've read a lot of the books recommended and struggled to finish. I often don't understand how they're insanely popular.

D.D.: Boost groups, and in this case, book tours.

Kat: Ok, we received a book you've sent us, odd it's not direct from the author though.

D.D: All legit. They send me the book in need of boosting, I'll share it with my team.

Kat: All out of the goodness of your heart. Right?

Evie: Can't wait, it sounds amazing @Dee.

How dare a mere reader ever query the Smut Mafia's reading tastes. I still giggle every time I hear the phrase. Children playing enforcers, pushing books. They've probably never stepped outside of the safety of a bedroom, yet put themselves on show to the world as influencers.

The_Smut_Mafia_Official

D.D.: Ladies, welcome to the new, upgraded chat. The freeloaders are still in the original group and probably haven't even noticed we've gone. Congrats you made it, I have a mission for our elite team.

Hearts and smileys pop up.

D.D.: Hit the free ebooks. I want authors from pre-2018, under twenty reviews–less is better. Around two hundred page books, no more than two fifty.
L.B.: On it. I have a few hidden on my device, ready to roll.
Kat: Question.
D.D.: Of course there is. What @Kat?
Kat: What is the criteria and aim of the above, please?
D.D.: Two-pronged approach. The rest know the deal, @Kat I'll message you rather than fill up the group. Is there anything else? Back with your contribution and list of books by Friday latest please, ladies.

Chat: Dee Dark & Kat.

D.D.: "What's with the third degree, Kat? Task set, simple. Why do you have to undermine me every time?"
Kat: I'm not undermining you, Dee. I'm trying to make sense of your request. It seems odd we're looking at older releases.
D.D.: Look, they're the lolly jar, treasure chest, whatever you want to call it. Those low-ranked books, authors either don't give a

fuck, or they're desperate to promote and don't have the bankroll to make it.

Kat: And if they're inclined to sign up? What's in it for you exactly?

D.D.: Just a few books. I can't afford to buy everything I read, so they offer products for the time spent.

Kat: Why not just pay you as a personal assistant?

D.D.: I can't PA. I need to watch my income, or they'll cut my benefits. It's either cash in hand, product, or gift cards. The usual is my Zon wishlist. They just pay for a suggested value provided and I receive whatever's on my list at the time.

Kat: I'm not here for freebies. It's not cheap for them as it is. If a book isn't doing well, why ask for more when they're already struggling to be visible?

D.D.: Author copies cost them fuck all–a few dollars. Most send directly from the printer. As for freebies, they're for team leaders only. I'll draw one member from a mini tour for a gift or direct from the author's book group competition, depending on what's on offer.

Kat: And if they don't cough up? Are they pressured?

D.D.: Most go out of their way to see their books in feeds. They're desperate for a book to go viral. Those viral books are often picked up by a publisher or even better, made for TV. Only we can give it to them.

Kat: Honestly, viral books are usually knock-offs. So, what happens if they don't play your game?

D.D.: You know those plots you help edit? The alpha reads you freely offer to jump in on? The books we promote are hard, with huge pre-orders and sales.

Kat: For your authors, sure.

D.D.: Where do you think they come from, hmm? Where do you think they end up?

Kat: In Gloria's novels?

D.D.: I thought you were smarter than that. Gullible. Look up Crazy Caz's plot group. It's who you're helping out. You honestly believed one author has over two hundred ready-to-go plot outlines? You can insert *ghostwriter* in your portfolio, hon. The work's there if you want it. You're surprisingly not too bad at this author crap.

Chapter Seventeen

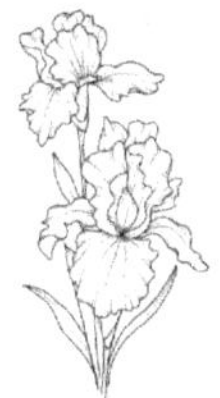

Kat

Present.

Night and day.

"Consider me a new team initiate. Explain targeting." Damon's question rattles me. It's close to home after rehashing my chat notes.

"Who? The books to plagiarize, or the mark to threaten promotion wise?"

"Whoa. Take a step back. The books to plagiarize? You mean the team is in on selection?"

Here we go, delving into the depths of the dirty laundry. "Yes and no. There's a criterion for both—so they're the same. The mark, as you call it, must be obscure. An author with under twenty reviews. A minimum of two years since release and negligible social media presence. A non-appealing cover hiding their work, or a category no one visits."

"Makes sense. If you're throwing a team of twenty on a review tour, you require a complete package. You'd not skimp on covers, so the book is overlooked." Adding to his notes, I'm aware Damon will look into this closely.

"As you know, after thirty days, new releases cease being recommended by algorithms unless they've hit the top one hundred. They disappear, making room for the next thing to feed into recommendations."

"Hence book tours of older releases, appearing on Instagram and Facebook."

I nod in agreement. He's been in the business long enough to witness changes firsthand, perhaps not join the dots. "The paid ads, certainly. Remember, our girls aren't a formal promotions company. They sit alongside some of the big names, playing bloggers. Book tours are illusory signups. The new reviews are arc reads. How do they benefit an author? You know the magic fifty-review threshold is a myth."

"I'm aware it's rejected. It's an urban legend, stuck with those lower on the totem pole. So, you didn't answer my question. They send you searching for fresh blood?" Kat shifts uncomfortably, paling. "I'm right, aren't I? They send the team for prey."

"Yes."

"How many Kat? How many do they prey on?" His rough voice sends a shiver down my spine.

"Only the ones who won't cough up money for their support. They're dead and buried before someone discovers their work was stolen."

Damon

"I'm a reader first. A curator of words. A collector of tomes that brought meaning to my life. I refuse to whisper sweet nothings and pad a fragile ego to boost a bank account. If a published product is lacking, be it traditional or independent—the author sold their words, it's a product, open for review." Kat's tone is matter-of-fact, she's adamant in her stance. I've quickly come to respect this aspect of her character.

"Regardless of creative license, publishing is a business transaction. You'd not fill a hamburger with rotten meat and expect the consumer to devour it without recourse or response. The same applies to the printed word. We all work and bleed for our income, being an artist does not exclude you from critique." I top up or coffee and settle in for a debate, pleased she's in fine form today.

Throwing herself from the chaise, Kat begins her all too familiar routine. "Ask yourself why? Why are there some absolute gems, beautiful works of literature, so eloquently written– profound voices with amazing skills–hidden away in the tombs? Heaven forbid a book is classed as erotica. Fine, we all want a little smut in our romance, but where is the percentage ridiculous and out of context? How do some escape the guillotine, while others are reported and buried? Are they such a threat to someone's ranking and crown, the elite are driven to destroy those worthy, terrified they'll take their title? It appears so."

She has a point. Often the best are squirreled away out of sight through no fault of the author, but it can't be this complex. "I'll play the wild card, and suggest this is rampant paranoia. To even contemplate there's a conspiracy so far-reaching they're controlling the masses, are you implying readers are blind to it?"

"Readers are knowledgeable." Notes fly from her hands, dropping onto my desk. She drags the visitor chair and balances precariously on the edge. "At some point, everyone grows up and moves away from fairytales. They may be darker, but as readers mature they seek reality and more intelligent reads. Imagine how infuriated those spending their hard-earned dollars on ebooks and paperbacks would be if they recognize it's manipulated?" I add another sugar to my coffee, absently stirring. "Surely it's not as deep as you're suggesting? It can't be occurring right under our noses. How many authors can you name, who are *honestly* submitting their work?"

"Maybe seven?"

"You have to be fucking joking. Out of millions of authors, you're suggesting there are only seven?"

"Seven mainstream easily recognized styles and names within indie, yes. Possibly one or two more, we're talking the top ranking romance tropes as a whole." Eyes downcast, I swear she's embarrassed by this train of thought.

"Holy shit. It can't be as bad as that." I fear she's close number-wise. The repertoire feels severely restricted in every trope at present.

"Top-ranked. Not the under fifty stars, or those overlooked who slide beneath the covers, so to speak. They're deserving of decent rankings; the rest are purchased via reviews and tours. Throw enough money and you'll make bank with the right connections."

"Fine, say I believe there's some truth to this scenario. I'm a new reader, point me in the direction I should be avoiding. Educate me. Treat me as if I know absolutely nothing about the book world. I've just discovered I can read book porn in pretty covers on a train, and no one realizes I'm getting off on it while they're listening to sports on their phones." I suppress a grin at the temptation to test this theory. I can't even contemplate traveling with a hard-on. How do women survive with the *wet panties* these novels claim to achieve?

Drawing in a deep breath, Kat scans through her notes, and

swaps to a provider website, bringing up the top one hundred books. "Pick a best seller. A quick read, a smut fest novella, and pay attention to those promoting." I watch with interest as she scrolls through the list, landing on number thirty-five this week. "Where have they come from? Their age bracket. Their connections to each other. Go through the reviews."

She thrusts her device at me, tapping the review link. "Do you see the pattern now? I beg you to tell me I'm wrong. There's a conspiracy to push a rotation of a few authors–under multiple pen names. They're recycling those same words, time and time again."

Kat taps on a new release, and a familiar name and title appear in the top forty. "This resembles a bad sitcom. If you don't succeed–working honestly, building and creating legitimate work —you recover, rework, and re-publish."

Nodding, Kat takes a sip of her coffee, groaning at the caffeine hit. "Words are infinite, are they not? So, answer me this, why must authors rehash the same books? If they've failed once, what's the point? On top of the first attempt, why use plot outlines others have previously published and flag your work?"

"They see potential in another's style? There's no copyright on plots or ideas. It's almost impossible to prove a concept has been stolen unless they're stupid enough to quote verbatim if it's what you're implying?."

"It's a morally ambiguous stance, suggesting you can't protect plots, honestly. Writers write, they're artists. Where is the joy of replicating, or reinventing someone else's work? It's the fairytale retelling all over again. Been there, done that, added a touch of gore or kink, and swapped in a trope. Too many live on the proceeds of public domain works, without touching on the theft from published works. Where's the joy of reading in this scenario?"

"None. It's comparable to watching reruns. Imagine only

having access to seven episodes of a television show, day in and day out."

"Exactly! Thank goodness someone else understands my insane soapbox. If words are infinite, why pray tell, don't authors utilize their god-given brains? You'd appreciate money spent on original content over…"

"Plagiarized work."

"There lies the crux of the matter and the source of outrage if readers cotton on to the scheme."

"Why haven't they? It's glaringly obvious. Based on your research, it's gone on for many years. Why aren't they outed for their behavior?"

Her pause makes me wonder if I've pushed too hard. Until now, I've felt like a dentist pulling teeth, one step at a time.

Her breath whooshes out, and she settles back into the chair. "Those involved constantly skirmish, running interference, generating drama and distraction. Haven't you noticed, as soon as one unbelievable offense occurs, it dies down, to be replaced by another?"

"Putting it like that, yes. It appears to be an ongoing issue. I still don't understand why. How is it productive to be at each other's throats constantly?"

"They benefit financially on all levels. The root of all evil remains the dollar. What does it cost to buy a promotion, get in, and get out, before anyone's the wiser? Before the general population picks up there's an issue, the pen name's retired, and their LLC's gone. Ghosted."

"Next step, they reappear, promote the book as a debut— a new release, an amazing new talent and polished as fuck. Tell me why no one queries the content?" With a head shake, her tight ponytail swings shoulder to shoulder, her frustration evident. Her coffee cup rattles on my desk, the plate below taking the brunt, as she pushes back to pace again,

"The original team and reader base has moved on, and the work is no longer recognized?" Adding to my notes, the depth of the deception is far more involved than I'd first assumed. "There are so few independents remaining who write their own words from scratch. Who plot, outline, edit, plan, and research. Old school authors who were taught by the best. They've read the classics, and have a firm grasp on the English language–cancel culture be damned. They write what needs to be written, not what they're told to create, to fit a market."

Nodding in agreement, Kat leans on the back of the chaise, picking at imaginary lint. "Those aren't the ones who'll be remembered. Not the outdated, overly sexualized covers. I cringe every time I see a style popular in traditional paranormal romance, used for indie Mafia. Add insult to injury, it's five years out of date. Don't they follow upcoming trends?"

Covers I know, and my research on indie cover trends was informative. "Unlike traditional publishing houses, these guys are small fry. Their alpha readers and teams appear to influence their model choices, trolling book sites and stalking their opposition—god knows why. Most are overused, or bare-chested young adults, reminiscent of 1970s porn with gold glitter topography."

Kat's reaction is priceless, stifling a giggle. "My kids aren't far off from most models age-wise. Creepy as fuck, and hilarious. I feel like a cougar ogling teenagers."

Epilogue

Damon

Present

"I'm watching the rats slink quietly from their midden—braver each day—believing they've won. Hesitant at first–taking small bites of the bait, they're increasingly confident. Bearing witness to their sheer audacity's entertaining." Kat chuffs at the analogy, I'm well aware she has a soft spot for the hairy little rodents and won't bait the ones inhabiting her basement.

"Hiding in plain sight has been their modus vivendi for too long—it's time to throw them to the dogs. The new generation of social media's clued in. They're not easily misled—for the most part. Scrupulous readers take immediate offense at anything untoward. Their call for action—their influence—supersedes anything the old order anticipated. A world-ending plague will do that."

"I was once told they didn't trust me." Her brittle voice pulls at my heartstrings inciting anger.

"Why the hell did you stay?"

"I didn't. I was on my way out the figurative door as they slammed it in a last-ditch effort to placate me. It was my final red flag. An outpouring of nothing substantial—defensive allegations. I was outrightly lied to, and on confrontation, the retribution was vicious–to put it lightly."

"On what grounds? What did you do for them to feel you were untrustworthy?"

"Nothing! Zero. I slaved at their beck and call for two years. The error in my way was to raise concerns when rules were broken–the potential to put their business at risk. Going to the source with your concerns was bitching. Who knew?"

At this stage, nothing surprises me with this group, despite the new revelations. "You took your concerns to your team leader in person?"

"I went one step further—directly to the author. Funny thing. The *'do as I say, not as I do,'* mentality is rife within this clique. Backbiting, bitching, underhanded behavior—call them on it, retaliate or question their loyalty–you're guilty of treason."

"You realize you're so much more than this, don't you? It's on them, not the reader, to rectify or atone for their sins. As far as sins go–I can't think of anything worse. Those stealing someone's story–there's no label for them." My concern is for Kat. "Are you emotionally prepared to survive the fire, already burning?" I reach for her hand, offering the only support I can provide. Her psychological scars–can't be erased with the few words in her outpouring. "It's not your guilt to carry."

"I'd debate it is mine. Subterfuge created a sick and twisted myriad of emotions within my soul. I believed I was at fault. I believed their way was the only way. I still second guess my path most days. Their undivided attention's addictive. They convinced me—brainwashed me. Worse, the same bloggers are now your newly debuted authors."

"And now? How do you still feel responsible?"

"Not just now—always—I knew it was wrong. There's no shade of gray; it's always black and white on paper. They're wrong. Corrupt. But they're damn good at manipulating and filling the cracks in times of need."

"A quick fix, surely?"

"A bandaid patching a volcano, nothing more. The magma continues to heat, the lava leaks slowly through the fissures—it never cooled—it just keeps running, finding places to drain into, and hide."

"What happens when you remove the bandaid?"

"They're not prepared for war—for the sacrosanct seals to shatter—nor mouths they believe are sewn shut in fear, to be unstitched, spilling their vile history." There's the woman I adore, the fight surges from within.

"Regardless of weaponry, you do understand they'll come back repeatedly under different guises?"

With an imperceptible nod, she acknowledges it won't be over. "Like vermin. I'd liken them to tiny red, german cockroaches, but the most symbolic vermin are rats–I prefer my rats over people most days so I'm not degrading my fuzzy friends as a comparison." Her breathy giggle at a repetitive joke lights up her face again. "Think of Roman era myth and legend. We are legiōn–the ultimate horde. Once it's in writing, in cyberspace, you have zero ability to reclaim and repossess the printed word. It exists for infinity."

"Vermin, pure and simple. I'd liken them to roof rats. The bastards are damn hard to get rid of–you know you'll need to eradicate them one day. I agree cockroaches are a better analogy. They're capable of surviving a nuclear holocaust."

"It's a lie, by the way." Her analytical mind kicks in–

the obscure references safely tucked away in the depths of a headspace darker than my own.

"The nuclear bomb idea?"

"Yep. Everything succumbs to fire, even those who climb high enough to observe from a throne. Such determined little bastards. Same as the bottom-feeding groups who return with a vengeance, breeding the next mutant generation. You can't kill them all off–a seed of sedition survives, hidden away." Her evil chuckle comes out of nowhere, raising the hairs on my neck.

"What's the point then? If they're only going to return strengthened, potentially immune to repercussions?" My biggest concern is retaliation–they'll decimate everyone close, to protect their lies.

"Pesticide, fire, big fucking boots—we'll throw it all at them, and no one will see it coming," she spouts with a maniacal grin. "And I'll sleep again at night, hopefully."

"Do you honestly believe this will achieve something? Won't they just rise reborn, or retaliate en masse?"

"Indie publishing may have crowned a few queens–without readers–it's just a house of cards, ready to fall. Time for the hidden to rise–be heard. Be seen. It's time we leveled the playing field again for all."

"So, Kat, what are we going to do next?"

"Set fire to it? Who knows? I'd not contemplated being placed in this position. It was never meant to be this way. All I know for certain is they better be wary. Prodding the dragon once too often means they've fueled the furnace." Kat hums a few familiar lines. "May we quote a great, and set fire to them all?"

"There's my girl! Time to blow up the corrupt, and create a truly diverse and honest new book world."

The end, for now.

Author's note

Thank you for taking the time to read. It's not plausible that anything so outlandish could occur under everyone's watchful eye–something to consider as you pick up your next read.

If you enjoyed this novella, please consider leaving a review. Alternatively, if you hated it, leave a review–every voice and opinion matters. If you publish fiction, you open yourself to criticism in every form. It's part and parcel of writing—love and hate go hand in hand, never take it personally.

Until next time.

Glossary

A brief list of terminology has been included for quick reference. If you are unfamiliar with any term, research is golden when reading. The new generation of readers learn everything from social media, and quite often, don't actually read the books in front of them. If they did, we would not be here.

Readers overall are intelligent—to assume otherwise, is vanity—never underestimate a reader. This is a key only, not a detailed or technical outline. The lookup option in the ebook feature connects to both internet search and dictionaries. It's a tool too often forgotten. Some readers may be less familiar with the included abbreviations.

Glossary of terms for the current generation.

This is a quick lingo decoder—not fluff or a page scam. Newbies slurp social slop, skip real reads. If they cracked spines, this mess wouldn't exist, right? Readers, they're razor-sharp—underrate 'em, regret it.

- . Ebook lookup: Web/dict ninja tool, dust it off.
- Indie: Self-pub mavericks or their word dumps.
- CMOS: Chicago Manual of Style—editors' sacred scroll for grammar, comp, rules.
- Content Warning: Author's red flag for gut-twisters. (Scrap "TW"—triggers are quirky, like clown terror.)
- NDA: Gag order.
- ARC: Pre-release tease.
- Street Team: Author's cheer mob for drop days.

• Boost Group: Comment conga line to hack algos (boomerangs bad).

• Wishlist: Amazon beg list—books for pity buys.

• ROAK: Surprise swag from public begs.

• Alpha Reader: Plot surgeon—big pic, chars, glue; edit-savvy pal.

• Beta Reader: Chapter sniper—flow fouls, glitches; NDA if not ride-or-die.

• ARC Reader: Hype drone for buffed drafts—not edit fodder.

• Word Choice: Ditch duds for dazzlers.

• Repetition: Loop killers—words on repeat? Axe 'em.

• Copy Editor: Word wizard—sharpens scribbles.

• Developmental Editor: Structure slayer—plot, build fixes.

• Line Editor: Dev mongrel.

• Proofreader: Typo terminator—no chit-chat.

• Editorial Assessment: MS takedown—style, speed, wins/losses.

• Pass: Edit circuit.

• MS: Raw word beast.

• Promo: Plug-and-play ads/graphics; stock pics shield sharers' hides.

• Annotations: Scribbles/highlights; now TikTok tease bait.

• Genre: Lit bin, e.g., romance.

• Trope: Genre spice, e.g., rom-suspense.

• Smut: Plot? Pfft—all bang.

• Spice: Steam gauge, hot as hell.

• Blurb: A snappy book tease—back-cover bait to hook suckers.

• Sock Puppet: Fake accounts puppeteered by authors for self-praise or rival sabotage.

• Plagiarism: Word theft—lifting plots, lines, or whole chunks without credit. Indie plague.

• Ghostwriter: Shadow scribe churning out "your" book for cash; credit? Optional.

• Review Bombing: Mob assault via fake low stars to tank a rival's rank.

• Ebook Scam: Free library hustle—page-stuffing or bot-reads for payout cheats.

• Booktok: TikTok's romance circus—hype machine for viral smut, often scripted.

• ARC Farm: Shady reviewer mills churning canned praise for promo perks.

• Gate (e.g., #Gate): Scandal suffix—publishing drama exposed, then buried.

• Black Hat Promo: Dirty tricks to game algos—fake engagement, bought buzz.

For those who speak traditionally acknowledged English:

•. Indie: Independently published/author.

• CMOS: The Chicago Manual of Style—editing/grammar bible.

• Content Warning: Author's alert for potential triggers. (Not "TW"—triggers are personal, e.g., clowns.)

• NDA: Non-disclosure agreement.

• ARC: Advanced reader copy.

• Street Team: Author-specific promo readers for releases.

• Boost Group: Group commenting to game algorithms (often counter productive).

• Wishlist: Amazon list of items (books) for gifting.

• ROAK: Random act of kindness—gift from public wishlist.

• Alpha Reader: Oversees development (plot, character); trusted editor-friend.

• Beta Reader: Chapter feedback on flow/inconsistencies; trusted/NDA.

• ARC Reader: Promo reviewer of polished book; not editor.

• Word Choice: Optimal terminology/synonyms.

• Repetition: Overused words/phrases.

• Copy Editor: Sharpens wording.

• Developmental Editor: Feedback on plot/build/structure.

• Line Editor: Hybrid developmental.

• Proofreader: Final typo hunt; no feedback.

• Editorial Assessment: Overall manuscript review (style, pace, issues).

- Pass: Editing read-through.
- MS: Manuscript/raw book.
- Promo: Pre-made posts/graphics for sharing (licensed photos indemnify sharers).
- Annotations: Notes/highlights; now social media hype tool.
- Genre: Literature category, e.g., romance.
- Trope: Subcategory, e.g., romantic suspense.
- Smut: Plotless sex.
- Spice: Sexual tension/heat level.

About the author.

Evie is the pen name of a writer who knows better than to enter the insane arena of independent publishing. The brainchild of a dare, clicking upload was possibly the strangest thing she's ever contemplated.

Trained in many things, master of none, now a stay at home fur mother, volunteer and avid reader.

Of the belief you're best suited to write what you know, it's what she was taught, after all, Evie first published as a student. Co-writing articles over the years, her shelves remain full of untold stories.

https://amazon.com/author/glh

Echelon Series: GLH, Genevieve L. Hughes (reverse harem).

Their Angel

Their Devil

Kestrel (tbc)

A Reader's Tale Series: writing as Evie Campbell

PuSh

BuRn

RiZe

HaCk (omnibus and bonus scene)

A Romancelandia Parody: GLH, Genevieve L. Hughes

Fallen Idols

Stratagem

Romancelandia (omnibus)

Opus: A Romancelandia Parody Finale

Reprieve Series shorts: GLH, Genevieve L. Hughes

Locked & Loaded

Shackled & Broken

Bound & Disarray

Reprieve (omnibus, includes additional scenes)

The Algal Bloom: fact, fiction or conspiracy.

Coming soon: Cry Wolf

Review Journals, notebooks and autograph books available on Amazon.

Social media links

https://linktr.ee/glh_books